RANDOM HOUSE

LARGE PRINT

LET'S JUST SAY IT WASN'T PRETTY

LET'S JUST SAY
IT WASN'T PRETTY
DIANE
KEATON

R A N D O M   H O U S E
LARGE PRINT

Cover design: Emily Harwood Blass
Cover photographs: Ruven Afanador

The Library of Congress has established a Cataloging-in-Publication record for this title.

ISBN: 978-0-8041-9443-3

www.randomhouse.com/largeprint

FIRST LARGE PRINT EDITION

Printed in the United States of America

10 9 8 7 6 5 4 3 2 1

This Large Print edition published in accord with the standards of the N.A.V.H.

TO ALL THE WOMEN WHO CAN'T GET TO RIGHT
WITHOUT BEING WRONG

CONTENTS

INTRODUCTION
WRONG IS RIGHT

I've always loved independent women, outspoken women, eccentric women, funny women, flawed women. When someone says about a woman, "I'm sorry, that's just wrong," I tend to think she must be doing something right. Take Diana Vreeland, the legendary editor in chief of **Vogue**. Vreeland was many things, but a classic beauty wasn't one of them. Her mother called her "my ugly little monster." Guess what? That didn't get in her way. Vreeland paraded around with a head of glossy pitch-black hair until the day she died, at age eighty-five. She defied every rule of aging gracefully. She thrived in the big-time world of Beauty, yet was not enslaved by it. Diana conjured a world where "you've gotta have style. It helps you get down the stairs. It helps you get up in the morning. It's a way of life. Without it you're nobody."

I respect women who aren't afraid to push the envelope, women who are inappropriate, women who do what you aren't supposed to. Women like Katharine Hepburn. Didn't she wear pants under a Chairman Mao tunic to the Academy Awards? No gown? No jewels? No stylist? No posing on the red carpet? Outrageous! And what about twenty-seven-year-old Lena Dunham, who has redefined what a star can look like. I think she's one of the most beautiful women on TV. Her HBO series **Girls** has hit a raw nerve with some reviewers. "One reason that **Girls** is unsettling is that it is an acerbic, deadpan reminder that human nature doesn't change," wrote Alessandra Stanley of **The New York Times**. "As funny and creative as her show may be," wrote Robert Bianco in **USA Today,** "there's little doubt **Girls** will be too explicit, too New York–specific, and too young-and-female-centric to appeal to everyone." That's the point: Why try to appeal to everyone?

I have a soft spot for women like Phyllis Diller. Remember her running after the garbage truck as it pulled away from the curb, yelling, "Am I too late for the trash?" "No," said the driver. "Jump right in!" I admire women like Joan Rivers, even though I can't count how many times she's hauled me before her Fashion Police. Look, it's hard not to love a woman who can laugh about the fact that an animated show once featured her as a vagina that had received too much plastic surgery. Joan, Phyllis, and Totie Fields were among the first to openly discuss their multiple cosmetic surgeries. It takes strength to fess up to your imperfections. People have asked me why I've never had work done. The truth is I respect women who have had work done just as much as I respect those who haven't. We're all just trying to get through the day.

In my early twenties I used to torture Woody with my insecurities: Would I ever be cast in a great movie? Would my slightly-but-definitely-noticeable crooked nose keep me from getting work? Looking back, I don't know how Woody put up with me. For a year and a half the only job I'd been cast in was the recurring role of a young woman running around in a tracksuit uttering "Hour After Hour won't wear off till the day is over." That's right, no one would hire me, except to sell underarm deodorant. I asked Woody if he thought I was crazy to keep flying to California to audition for films like Anthony Newley's **Summertree** only to lose out to actresses like Brenda Vaccaro. And even if I landed one of those roles, would I ever have a career? Woody told me I didn't have to worry. You're funny, he said, and funny is money. I looked at him and thought, Is this guy nuts? Funny women told jokes. I wouldn't know a joke if it hit me in the face. Funny women knew where the punch line came. I was always fumbling for the right thing to say. Funny women like Joan Davis from **I Married Joan** had a great career playing fall-down clowns with names like Flossy Duff. Funny women were comedic geniuses like Carol Burnett, or Ruth Buzzi of **Laugh-In,** who made herself look pretty awful with her most inspired character, Gladys Ormphby, an ugly spinster whose hair was pulled into a bun secured by a hairnet knotted in the middle of her forehead. Not exactly what you'd call attractive. Joan, Carol, and Ruth took funny to the edge of a cliff and they weren't afraid to fall off. That's when I understood what Woody was talking about. It's why Phyllis Diller worked into her nineties and Joan Rivers is still a force to be reckoned with. It's why I love funny women. They make funny beautiful.

Speaking of fearless and original, what about Lady Gaga, who has worn outfits that look like a chicken nugget and a feather duster? Love that. And Rihanna, the black Madonna, who reinvents her style and image with every album. To me, the most beautiful women are independent women like Angelina Jolie, Anna Magnani, fierce and sassy Jennifer Lawrence, Georgia O'Keeffe alone in the desert, Laurie Simmons (Lena Dunham's mother), Cindy Sherman front and center in her photographs, Barbra Streisand with her untouched nose, strong Kathryn Bigelow, defiant Kate Moss, Grace Coddington and her orange hair, Louise Brooks and her black bob, Françoise Hardy, unstoppable Hillary Clinton, brilliant Tina Fey, fearless Joan Didion, and and and and . . . each found her place in the world. Each has her own style, her own voice, her own independence, her own stamp, her own method, her own wrong that she's made right.

Just yesterday Dexter, my eighteen-year-old daughter, found a story online called "Top 10 Female Celebrities Who Are Ugly No Matter What Hollywood Says" by someone named Valdez_Addiction.

"Mom. Mom. Come over here." I ran to the computer and there was a picture of Number One, Angelina Jolie, with this assessment: "She looks like Skeletor from He-Man. Sorry Brad, you could have done much better than this stick figure." Valdez_Addiction slammed Number Four, Reese Witherspoon, with this: "What can I say about this genetic mistake that you can't already see? Between that chin and that fore-head that she finally realized she needed to cover, I'm still amazed she even has a career much less being voted beautiful by people magazine." Dexter kept scrolling, and there was the fifth-ugliest female celebrity no matter what Hollywood says, Diane Keaton.

How this chick got a lead role in anything is beyond me. And I know what you're thinking. It's not because she's old as dirt and they still try to give her sexy roles. She's even ugly in the Godfather when she was young.

Old as dirt. Wow. I went to my bathroom and looked in the mirror. "Let it go, Diane. No wallowing in self-pity. You have a family. You have a brother and two sisters. You have a daughter and a son. You have work. You have friends. You can feel. You can think, up to a point. Your legs walk, your arms swing. You can see. Seeing is believing. Seeing is the gift that keeps giving. It's much more engaging than being seen. That's the bottom line, Diane. . . . Get over yourself. Listen to your friend Daniel Wolf's advice—want what you have."

Daniel's not wrong, but he's not entirely right. It isn't quite that simple. I wish it were, but beauty is more complicated than that. Let's get real: Does anyone know a woman over fifty who hasn't taken a long hard look in the mirror and recited some version of this not so pretty monologue? "Diane, I've got some bad news. No matter what you do, no matter how much Restylane and Botox, no matter how many face-lifts and arm lifts and body lifts (good idea, why not get the whole package taken care of in one fell swoop and call it a day); no matter how many brow lifts, thigh lifts, breast lifts, breast reductions, breast augmentations, tummy tucks, nose jobs, eye jobs, cheek implants, or chin implants; no matter how many chemical peels, laser skin resurfacings, spider vein treatments, permanent makeup applications (permanent sounds good), liposuctions, hair replacements, dermal filler polylactic acid treatments, dermal filler PMMA treatments, dermal filler polyalkylimide treatments (that's a lot of dermals), calcium hydroxylapatite (whatever that is), etc., etc. . . . Are you listening? No matter what you do you will still be a sixty-seven-year-old woman on the downhill slide."

So, what is beauty if it isn't Angelina Jolie and Reese Witherspoon? Why do we try to pin it down by categorizing it as absolute? Why limit it at all? Why is classic beauty the gold standard? Why is **gold** the gold standard? And what is "classic"? What's precious about precious stones? Why are diamonds a girl's best friend? Don't tell me what beauty is before I know it for myself.

These old-as-dirt days have one advantage: I've learned to see beauty where I never saw it before. But only because my expectations are more realistic. My favorite part of my body is my eyes. Not because of their color and God knows not because of their shape, but because of what they see. When I was in my twenties and thirties I wanted my appearance to be more interesting than the beauty that surrounded me. It was a fool's folly.

On my fifteenth birthday my dad told me I was becoming a pretty young lady. Mom said I had a pretty smile. One of my teachers complimented me on my pretty new dress. I was old enough to understand that pretty was a poor cousin to beautiful. Pretty was the stuff of being friendly but not being friends. Pretty was the right dress from Bullocks department store, not a beatnik tunic with black tights and a beret. Pretty was Sandra Dee, easy and light. Pretty fades. Beautiful was Natalie Wood, deep like the ocean. I knew this because on the cliffs of Laguna Beach I cried from the sheer wonder of what I saw. Beautiful makes you come back for more. It makes you ask questions. It's vast, unknowable, and magnificent. That's part of its power. It makes you think about the experience it's giving you. That's when I knew what I wanted. I've been chasing it ever since.

If we're lucky we have a long time to consider what beauty means. One thing I know, there is no beauty without pain. Beauty flourishes on sorrow. It's enriched by the knowledge that life is fleeting, sometimes cruel, and often ends without resolution. That's what makes beauty deep. Marilyn Monroe's insecurity explains her continuing appeal. It wasn't just her pretty face. It was the depth of her sad experience. Without living through the journey from orphan to goddess with a breathless voice, would she have become a legend? In the complexity of her suffering lies the universality of her appeal. How did Picasso come to see the scope of Marie-Thérèse's riveting head and shape it? I'll tell you how: through loving her, living with her, and seeing her as both ugly and magnificent. Because of his sculptures, Marie-Thérèse emerged as a symbol of unsightly, frightening, even hideous but also, I have to say, complete beauty.

When I was growing up I had a hard time doing much of anything right. Dad was always harping, "Diane, how many times do I have to tell you, don't stand in front of the open refrigerator, you're wasting electricity." Or "Diane, use your noggin. That's what happens when you forget your lunchbox in the car. You don't get lunch." And every single night at the dinner table: "For God's sake, Diane, keep your mouth closed when you chew." There was always something interfering with getting things right: a question (the wrong kind), a hesitancy, and always, always the mangling of my sentences, the stammers, the ums, the you-knows, the oh-wells, the I-don't-knows. I was inept, inexact, and imprecise. I would never have believed you if you had told me that this ineptness would help me later on, but somehow it did and I made my way.

Mom, on the other hand, taught me there was beauty in the imperfect. She would jot down words of wisdom and leave them on my desk. Things like "You don't have to be perfect to be beautiful." "Walk in power." "Find a reason to love yourself every day." "Only you can decide if things are right or wrong." "Buy yourself a gift for just being you." "Honor yourself, Diane. You deserve it." "Laugh at your friend Leona for making fun of your face." When I was a senior at Santa Ana High School, these words of wisdom, while well intended, seemed stupid. Walk in power? Laugh because someone tells you you're ugly? Please. "Only you can decide if things are wrong or right"? Okay, but how?

Look, I get how Valdez and others might see me: the woman hiding under her hat to be seen.

I know it might sound disingenuous at best and whiny at worst to complain about what I find in the mirror. But I'd be lying if I told you my mornings don't start with self-doubt, and you wouldn't believe me anyway. Besides, when I think about beauty I mean something much bigger than a face in the mirror or a photograph of an undeniably gorgeous woman or even some Internet story about Hollywood's ten ugliest female celebrities. I'm talking about that overwhelming feeling you get when you stand on a cliff and look out at the ocean. I'm talking about Phyllis Diller chasing the garbage truck or Joan Rivers getting in the first laugh about herself.

Or Katharine Hepburn in her tunic on the red carpet. Or Lady Gaga in her egg. Or Diana Vreeland's wise words about style helping you get down the stairs. I'm talking about finding whatever works for you to get out the door every day. I'm talking about the flaws that eventually take on a life of their own. The ineptness that makes you who you are. I'm talking about women who make us see beauty where we never saw it; women who turn wrong into right.

PRISONERS ON MY WALL

As I throw my coat on the chair, I see Alexander Gardner's 1865 portrait of Abraham Lincoln hanging on my living room wall. My first impression of President Lincoln came from a book I checked out of the Bushnell Way Elementary School library, **Abe Lincoln: Log Cabin to White House,** by Sterling North. In it President Lincoln fought to free the slaves. He was a great man who paid the ultimate price. Mr. North described President Lincoln as unsightly, even homely. To a ten-year-old girl, that meant President Lincoln was ugly. I didn't understand how an ugly man could become the president of the United States. Gardner's photograph, taken just days before Lincoln was shot in Ford's Theatre, contradicts North's description of a man who got shortchanged in the looks department.

Dominated by a pair of eyes set in darkness, Lincoln's face is magnificent. His left eye, engaged by what it sees, looks out with endless empathy, while his right eye tells a story that is harder to comprehend. The bottom half of his face, framed by two deep lines, singles out his prominent nose, but it's those eyes, particularly the left eye, the caring eye, the engaged eye, that is so compelling. Or is it? As my own eyes drift across Lincoln's wide forehead, I look back into the right eye, the one drawn toward reflection, and you know what I see? I see the darkness of a great calling.

Did President Lincoln's face become magnificent because he accepted a grave responsibility that would lead to a tragic end? Or was it the angle of Mr. Gardner's pose, the light, the patina? Was it good luck or a fortunate mistake? After living with Mr. Lincoln's portrait for several years, I've come to this conclusion: his beauty, like the hidden cast of his right eye, became identifiable only after I included "unsightly" as a possible way of describing a beautiful face.

Sharing wall space with Abraham Lincoln are

forty-seven other portraits of men I've collected over twenty-five years. I call them my prisoners. There's Robert Mapplethorpe's portrait of the artist Francesco Clemente, who presents his hands from under a black coat. There's Marion Robert Morrison's face before he became John Wayne. On the bottom left, Tony Ward is painted with mud. His hands frame his eyes. Maybe he's sick of looking out from under the dirt. Maybe he doesn't want to be painted into a shadow; maybe he's tired of being Herb Ritts's favorite model. The face of the Russian revolutionary and poet Vladimir Mayakovsky stares out in shaved-head resistance. He brings up longings. I'd carry his coattails. I'd be his lackey. Next to the kitchen door, Elvis Presley is sticking his tongue into a young woman's mouth. I never understood why he made millions of girls cry until I saw Albert Wertheimer's **Kiss** in an ad for Sam Shepard's play **Fool for Love**.

Which brings up Sam Shepard, who is framed dead center among the other prisoners on my wall. I was thirty-one when I went to a matinee of Terrence Malick's **Days of Heaven** at Cinema 1 on Third Avenue between Fifty-ninth and Six-tieth Streets in Manhattan. The movie seemed to glide through a brilliantly lit travelogue until Sam Shepard walked onto the screen and took my breath away. His face bore the imprint of the

West in all its barren splendor. For years, I followed Sam's life from the safety of distance, a fan's distance. He was the playwright of **Buried Child** and **True West.** He worked with Bob Dylan. He was married. He fell out of marriage, and into love with Jessica Lange. He wrote, "When you're looking for someone, you're looking for some aspect of yourself, even if you don't know it. What we're searching for is what we lack." And that's the way it was. Some aspect of him was an aspect in me, an aspect I hadn't developed, something I lacked. Or so I thought.

As life would have it, Sam slipped into the background until ten years later, when I inadvertently came across his face on a fifty-cent eight-by-ten glossy I bought at the Rose Bowl swap meet. The photograph was not exceptional except for one thing: Sam's face. That damn face. A day doesn't go by without a glance his way.

Gary Cooper also came to me in motion, but he wasn't beautiful. What he was, was old. I saw him walking a dusty town's deserted street toward four killers in Fred Zinnemann's 1952 motion picture **High Noon**. The movie was told in "real time," a time where events happened at the same rate that my ten-year-old eyes experienced them. Everything about the movie seemed super real. On Gary Cooper's wedding day to Grace Kelly, he had a choice: he could either ride into the horizon with his pretty new bride or stay and face the killers. As a girl I didn't think about Gary Cooper's looks, or the difference between Grace Kelly's age and his. I didn't care. Would he ever see her again? Would he die? Did he have to be so brave? I remember their goodbye. I remember Tex Ritter singing "Do Not Forsake Me, Oh My Darlin'." I remember crying. Looks weren't the issue. Courage was. I didn't know that courage was a form of beauty, but I must have felt it.

Imagine my surprise when I discovered Cecil Beaton's photograph of a thirty-year-old drop-dead-gorgeous Gary Cooper. Beaton did more than document the awe-inspiring good looks; he somehow captured Gary Cooper's awkward lack of calculation, his sweetness. Sometimes I compare the portraits of Gary Cooper and Sam Shepard. One photograph is of a man my age, still alive, still Sam. The other is an image of a legend I never met. Gary Cooper's photograph is the work of an artist. Sam Shepard's photograph is just another glossy eight-by-ten. Both, however, set off memories of milestone moments in movie theaters.

John Wayne's is the youngest, most irresistible face framed behind glass. It's ironic that he would become the ultimate symbol of the American male. There's no hint of aspiration in his expression. He seems almost perplexed by the idea that someone is taking his picture. How could a football player from Glendale have imagined donning a big old ten-gallon hat for some guy with a Rolleiflex dangling around his neck? Before Gary Cooper and Sam Shepard, it was John Wayne, the Duke, who would walk through the western landscape and into the heart of Joan Didion, who describes him best: "We went three and four afternoons a week, sat on folding chairs in the darkened Quonset hut which served as a theater, and it was there, that summer of 1943 while the hot wind blew outside, that I first saw John Wayne. Saw the walk, heard the voice. Heard him tell the girl in a picture called **War of the Wildcats** that he would build her a house, 'at the bend in the river where the cottonwoods grow.' As it happened I did not grow up to be the kind of woman who is the heroine in a Western, and although the men I have known have had many virtues and have taken me to live in many places I have come to love, they have never been John Wayne, and they have never taken me to that bend in the river where the cottonwoods grow. Deep in that part of my heart where the artificial rain forever falls that is still the line I wait to hear."

All three men came and went as they walked through time on the screen. All three acted out stories written for the entertainment of the masses, particularly women like me. All three are icons. Now they're incarcerated on my wall, where their beauty continues to evolve. Gary Cooper, John Wayne, and Sam Shepard still take me to Joan Didion's "bend in the river where the cottonwoods grow." They still give me hope for a house that can never be—a home that exists only in my dreams.

Warren Beatty is not one of the prisoners on my wall. He is a person I loved in real time, not reel, and not in a photograph. Real-life Warren was a collector's item, a rare bird. He lived in a three-room, eight-hundred-square-foot penthouse on top of the Beverly Wilshire hotel. Littered with books and scripts, the place was not fancy. Yet he owned an unfinished Art Deco estate on a hilltop, and he claimed he was going to make it his home. He was always late and always meeting people, and always, always, always working on a script. He had aspirations I couldn't begin to contemplate. You have to remember, I was Annie Hall. At that point I was happy to act in movies, not produce, star, and direct them while contemplating a political career. One moment Warren was stunning, especially from the right side; the next, I couldn't figure out what all the fuss was about. These variables kept me curious. Was he a beauty or wasn't he?

Yes. Warren was a beauty. That stood out

with particular intensity during our bittersweet breakup. And wouldn't you know it, it revolved around a photograph I saved but couldn't find to put on my wall.

I was in Germany working on George Roy Hill's **The Little Drummer Girl** in the early eighties. It was a difficult shoot. Picking me to play a British actress who finds herself embroiled in the Israeli-Palestinian conflict was bad casting. Picture the poster: a silhouette of Diane Keaton with unusually well-endowed curves leaning against a semiautomatic rifle. Today you can buy it on eBay for a dollar ninety-nine, which is just about what **The Little Drummer Girl** made at the box office.

No matter how hard I tried to look butch holding an Uzi assault weapon or to master an English accent, I failed. To make matters worse, Warren and I weren't speaking. On my days off, I would wander around Munich feeling sorry for myself. One Sunday at a flea market I came across a big picture book on the films of Warren Beatty. I bought it. Back in the hotel room, I cut out a picture of Warren from **Bonnie and Clyde,** folded it into small squares, put Warren in my jacket pocket, and brought him to work the next day. Before a particularly emotional scene, I took it out, unfolded Warren, and touched his face with my fingers. When I put my lips to his, all those months of straining for a crumb of feeling came flooding back. That's what Warren's face on the page of a broken-down book printed on cheap paper did to me before I shot a scene from **The Little Drummer Girl**.

At some point I lost the photo. In a way, I'm glad I did. It doesn't belong with my other convicts. Warren was not a fantasy to ponder. I knew him well. He was not a mystery to contemplate. Sometimes I wonder if he enjoyed his beauty. Did he like what the mirror reflected? He knew that his pretty face, set on that masculine body, blessed with a great mind, would continue to seduce legions of women with incredible success decade after decade after decade. But did he know that, like all gifts, it came with a price tag?

A question for Warren, and all of my inmates: When did they begin to worry about time's effect on their faces, if they did at all? What was it like for fifty-one-year-old Gary Cooper to see his close-ups in **High Noon**? What was it like for "the Duke"? Tom Cruise, who turned fifty-one recently, is on the eve of losing his looks. Brad Pitt is forty-nine. Johnny Depp is fifty. How are they dealing with the first signs of loss? Warren Beatty, now seventy-six, and his pal Jack Nicholson, at seventy-six, have let it go. They're over the hump. Al Pacino, too. Maybe letting go is the only graceful thing to do. My face was never in the same league as my prisoners'. There's nothing extra . . . ordinary about it. It's okay. Not bad. Normal. I'm a pretty, good-looking woman. In a way, my loss has been a gain. Someone has to play the hopes and wishes of women in my generation. I was never a shocking standout like Warren. I was no Julie Christie. I was, as one person described me . . . "a washed-out Ali McGraw."

My daughter, Dexter, has never heard of Gary Cooper. She knows Jack Nicholson because I made a movie with him. I was a little surprised when my friends Sandra Shadic and Lindsay Dwelley, both in their early thirties, told me they'd never heard of Gary Cooper, either. When I showed Sandra Cecil Beaton's photograph, yes, she found Cooper beautiful, but not in a significant way. Lindsay agreed that Cooper had a kind of masculine appeal. Dexter shrugged when I showed her. I guess it's a question of how you see people, how you picture time and place. Maybe it's also a question of age. For example, on Dexter's list of the twenty-five hottest men, Taylor Lautner is one, Justin Bieber two, Zac Efron three, and Robert Pattinson rounds off four. She did throw in one oldie: thirty-six-year-old Orlando Bloom. To prove that these five men were the sexiest men on earth, she showed me a cluster of tweets from other girls who had their own ideas about the hot twenty-five:

"Number seven should be switched with
	Justin Bieber."
"awesome list, when i first told my
	friends how hot Tom Felton was they
	didn't believe me, and now im like,
	hahahahah."
"good list i think zac efron is the hottest."
"robert Pattison is the BEST."
"Taylor and Robert are both Gorgeous."
"Alright no offense to zac efron but this is
	a disgrace to taylor lautners name! he
	should have been number 1!!!!"
"You should add Oliver Jackson Cohen
	too. He is so handsome!"
"I admired most Robert Pattinson."
"Taylor Lautner is Soooo Hot. He is
	Number 1 too me. i love him so much."

Poor Orlando Bloom didn't even make the cut.

Once it was me looking at my number one really neat coolest ever man, Fess Parker, also known as Davy Crockett, wearing his coonskin cap on the back of a Kellogg's Corn Flakes box. Later it was a signed photograph from James Garner, then starring in **Maverick,** and another from Edd (Kookie) "Lend Me Your Comb" Byrnes from **77 Sunset Strip**. After that it was James Dean and Marlon Brando. Then Jack

Nicholson in **One Flew over the Cuckoo's Nest**. Later it was the crumpled photograph of a man I'd once loved cut from an old paperback movie-star book. Now it's forty-eight men hammered to my wall.

Other women collect men, too; they must. Maybe their detainees are stuck inside journals, or posted on their Facebook page, or Scotch-taped to the corner of a bathroom mirror. It's all the same, right? Well, not exactly. I've probably taken it a little too far, what with a floor-to-ceiling wall filled with men's faces. At least I don't play favorites: not Marlon Brando, not Gary Cooper, not Matt Dillon, or Paul Newman, Morgan Freeman, Ryan Gosling, Adrien Brody, not even Halle Berry's catch of all time, Olivier Martinez, or my new addition, Jeremy Renner . . . no, no, no, all get equal time. Collectively they come and go in soft and sharp focus, in black and white, and color, too. They are the promise of eternity and the fun of fantasy. Sometimes they look into the wonder of my eyes. Sometimes they glide their fingers across the outline of my lips and say the same line over and over: "Diane, Diane, look at you. You're beautiful. Do you know that? Can you see your beauty through the light in my eyes, Diane? Look. Listen to me: I will make a home for you in a place where the cottonwoods grow."

Once, in the early 1970s, I passed John Wayne on my way to an audition for the TV series **Mc-Millan & Wife** at the Paramount lot. He seemed to be in a hurry. That was it. Several years ago I ran into Francesco Clemente. He charmingly mentioned his new project: painting portraits of interesting women like Toni Morrison, Fran Lebowitz, and Renée Fleming. Hoping that he found me fascinating too, I waited for his call. Needless to say, there is no portrait of Diane Keaton. I've met Tony Ward the model. He was polite. I made four movies with Sam Shepard, a mesmerizing man, but I never really got to know him. Just as well.

In the end, there are two ways of seeing male beauty. Real or imagined. There's the looking-in way and the being-seen way. There's the man himself and the man I've made up. I'm guilty of one, and proud of the other.

Last year I went to the White House Correspondents' Dinner in Washington, D.C., where I met Wolf Blitzer and hugged Colin Powell. I was in the same room with President Obama as he gave his speech. Michelle sat next to him. It was hard to get my mind around the reality of being in the presence of so many of the most powerful people in the world—that is, the people who run it and the journalists who tell the stories that help us assimilate the information.

The next day I took a tour of the White House, including the Situation Room, which I found surprisingly unassuming. All those big decisions in such a small room. I saw pictures of Hillary Clinton and Leon Panetta sitting around the television sets as they watched the Navy SEALs land in Osama bin Laden's compound in Abbottabad. I walked over to the Corcoran to look at the paintings, and the National Gallery, too. As the sun began to set, I dropped by the Lincoln Memorial. It was cold when I got out of the car. From a distance I saw the monument lit from inside. As I got closer, there he was again, this time nineteen feet high, resting his arms on a marble chair. The great man with the unsightly face, all alone. Thank God for that face and those eyes, one looking out for man's best interests, the other searching within for solutions to impossible conflicts. I gasped in awe. Here was the depth of beauty. And here were those same eyes looking out from inside a national monument to the memory of a great man.

COR-
RECTIONS

The face is our most important sensory organ. It is a compound so diverse and varied that there are no two faces alike. Yet we all share its five senses. For example, our noses take in smells. We hear with our ears. We taste with our mouths and touch with our lips. We see (one of my favorites) from our eyes. The face includes things like hair, foreheads (one, not two), eyebrows (two, not one, with as many as seven hundred hair follicles on each brow). We have one pair of lips, thirty-two teeth (for the most part), skin (a vital organ), and one chin. These make up the façade of the average human head. But the most amazing aspect of the face is its ability to show expression. More than anything, our face identifies who we are.

I was eleven when I first looked into the bathroom mirror and felt disappointment. I couldn't exactly pinpoint my dissatisfaction. I wasn't ugly. But I wasn't Doris Day. Doris Day was my idol. She sang hits like "Que Sera, Sera" and "Secret Love," which won the Academy Award for Best Original Song in my favorite movie, **Calamity Jane.** Played by Doris Day, Calamity Jane was shiny and blond. Pressing my face against the mirror, I tried to imagine what I would look like with yellow hair. That's when my younger sister Robin (always annoying) started banging on the door. "Open the door, Diaps," she demanded. (Short for Die Dee Diapers.) "What are you doing in there?"

"None of your business," I said.

"Get out. I need to use the bathroom now."

I put my fingers in my ears, cocked my head in an attempt to mimic Doris Day's adorable mannerisms and said, "This town ain't big enough. Not for me and that frilled-up, flirtin', man-rustlin' petticoat."

"Mom!! Diane won't get out of the bathroom."

Unlocking the door, I had a dim awareness that the best thing to do about wishing I was gun-toting, sarsaparilla-drinking Doris Day was just don't. Don't wish for something you can't have. But I did anyway.

Every month I ran to the mailbox to see if Mom's subscription to **McCall's** magazine had arrived. In its pages I learned that Maybelline Cake Mascara was "the first modern eye cosmetic for everyday use." I discovered the theory of "Before and After," which meant there was a before me and the hope of an after me. This was good news. I was excited for Tangee cosmetics when it presented "Bright 'n Clear," a lipstick "for lips men long to kiss again and again and again." Testimonials from real women, in real life, confirmed that Bright 'n Clear went on easily and magically transformed into the perfect shade for you.

I'll never forget the day our next-door neighbor Laurel Bastendorf said, "Diane, you know who you look like?"

"Doris Day?" I asked.

"Oh no, this is far better. You look like Amelia Earhart, the famous woman pilot whose plane went down over the Pacific—you know, the national heroine? You could be mistaken for her daughter." Amelia Earhart? A flier? What happened to Doris Day, or even Debbie Reynolds? I ran home and got out the **Encyclopaedia Britannica,** where I found a picture of what appeared

to be a man in a leather Dwight Eisenhower–
type windbreaker. I didn't want to look like a
man. Still, I couldn't deny the obvious similarities. She, too, had a high forehead; her eyes also
slanted down, not up; and, of course, her face
was the essence of plain.

The slights continued to mount. Even un-
intended insults were humiliating, like the day
I asked Mom if my eyes were green. "They're
hazel. You know that, Diane." But the next time
I looked in Mom's magnified mirror, I discovered my eyes weren't hazel. They were gray, and
they would always be gray. What was I going to
do? I couldn't change the color of my eyes. Even
more troubling were the folds of skin that hung
down over my drooping eyelids. Pressing on, I
focused on what Mom referred to as my lovely
auburn hair. **Webster's** defined Auburn as a city
in Alabama, and also as the color copper, rus-
set, or red. There was no red, or any of its variables, in my hair. Was Mom kidding? The more
I looked at my face, the more determined I was
to buy a Doris Day mask. But what if there was
no such a thing as a Doris Day mask? Besides, I
couldn't wear a mask to school every day. What
was I going to do?

I'll never forget the day I overheard Mom's best
friend Willie Blandin discuss aging issues with
Mom. With a Camel cigarette hanging from her

red-hot lips, Willie inhaled deeply before saying these unforgettable words: "Dot, listen to me: the way to avoid bags under your eyes is to do eye exercises on a daily basis." Maybe that was it; maybe that was the way to pick up my sagging eyes.

I admired Willie not just because she had a million beauty tips—like "Always style your hair with a curl that flicks either up or under" and "Believe in pink." Like Bette Davis, Willie had a high forehead. Her solution? Bangs. She tried to convince Mom to cut **hers** as well, claiming they would give Dot (she always called Mom Dot) a more youthful appearance. Mom would have none of it. For me, the opportunity to reduce the square footage of my forehead seemed brilliant. The problem? Mom was holding the scissors that cut my bangs. The results? Tragic. Think Depression-era bowl cut. Think Moe of the Three Stooges. What little hair I had—and I didn't have a lot—had been destroyed. Mom's response: "Diane, stop complaining and be proud. You have a lovely forehead, like Bette Davis." Bette Davis?! Sorry, but enough with Bette Davis. Oh, and just to reiterate, Willie wasn't wrong about bangs. To give credit where credit is due, it was Willie who introduced me to the idea of "Corrections."

I was fourteen when I first jotted down a few

in my "Dear Diary." It was August 8, 1960. This is what I wrote:

1. Sleep with a bobby pin stuck on top of my nose. Tilt it to the left where the bulb is fat, by fat I mean swollen to the extreme. If pressed on a regular basis the bulb will eventually be squeezed out of existence.

2. Spend time practicing a series of smiles. Part of "smile time" must be attended to by exercising the sincerity of my feelings. The best location is in the back seat of Mom's station wagon where I can see myself in the rearview mirror, free from Robin's dim-witted remarks.

3. Exercise my eyes for 30 minutes a day. Open them as wide as possible, then shut them tight, at least 24 times every 60 seconds. In addition, swing them back and forth faster than the speed of light. This kind of to and fro motion, which **McCall's** magazine describes as "swaying," will make them appear wider set apart. By combining these two exercises my eyes will actually become larger. Don't forget to try exercising in Civics class, where

Mrs. Clark is frequently distracted, but watch out for Mr. Barnett in Spanish Two, he's no fool.

4. Today I tried "smile time" on Dawn Utley and Dale Finney by looking off into the distance with a happy-faced grin. No response. After I finished my eye exercises in the girls' bathroom I spotted Dave Garland, so I leaned against his locker and pretended to be lost in thought. As I slowly turned my face to his and smiled with a glow that came from the heart, he said, "Hey, Diaps, what's the matter? Did somebody die? You look weird."

5. This morning the bobby pin on my nose left a mark that took a half hour to wear off. I've decided to buy some wooden clothespins. They're much more gentle. I asked Mom if I could eat my Cheerios in the bedroom 'cause I needed more alone time. If she knew what I was up to, it would be curtains, but the risk is worth it. Besides, I'm sick of listening to boring Bob Crane on the radio.

Mom let me wear lipstick in ninth grade. It was so much fun. But one day Willie Blandin took a long, hard look at my face and said, "Diane, listen to me. Now that you've started wearing lipstick, you can never go back. I'm not steering you wrong. Those lips of yours are going to dry up and disappear into nothing more than slits unless you have an ever ready supply of lipstick in your pocket. Welcome to womanhood, young lady." She scared the hell out of me, until Maria Gusman, Willard Junior High School's only female janitor, commented on how pretty I looked and inquired about the color of my lipstick. Thrilled, I thought of Willie in gratitude, and vowed to never leave the house without a tube of lipstick in my pocket. In her honor I shared my knowledge of Tangee's "Many Mini Colors" with Maria. I also suggested that Maria might consider the new set of Revlon's "frosty" colors for women with darker complexions.

Eye makeup at school was a different story. Willie supported it. Mom was firm: no eye makeup. How ridiculous. I mean, come on, it was 1960. Models like Twiggy, Jean Shrimpton, and Penelope Tree never appeared on the cover of fashion magazines without plenty of eye makeup. Plus, "the Shrimp," **Vogue**'s "face of the moment," was only a few years older than me. Mom finally caved during my junior year and allowed me to spend my salary from Newberry's five-and-ten-cent store on a Maybelline eye kit.

Sitting in my bedroom, I read the entire Maybelline eyeliner-application pamphlet. First: with Maybelline's soft eyebrow pencil, I was told to draw a narrow line across the upper eyelids, at the base of lashes, adding a short upstroke at the outer corner. Then, and only then, would I be ready to soften the line with my fingertips. Next: use short, light upward strokes of Maybelline's eyebrow pencil to form beautiful expressive brows, then taper lightly at the outer end to soften the effect. This was fun. I liked the whole soften-the-effect concept. Maybelline suggested I buy their smooth mascara, too. It would further enhance my eyes. For an extra touch of mysterious eye beauty, the pamphlet added, it would be wise to blend a bit of Maybelline eye shadow on the upper lids. The instructions said it would "bring out the unsuspected loveliness" of my eyes.

My makeup bonding with Willie continued throughout high school. As a bona fide member of "Club Willie," I was privy to some of the more extreme remedies for facial woes. According to her sources (whatever that meant), Marilyn Monroe was nineteen when her agent, Mr. Johnny Hyde, advised her to have a slight bump of cartilage removed from her bulbous nose. Bulbous? Oh my God. Marilyn Monroe had a bulbous nose, too?! Willie must have made that up. A nose job? No way. Willie also described Ann Miller's botched nose job. "Who's Ann Miller?" I asked. Shocked, Willie informed me that Ann Miller had starred in **Easter Parade** with Fred Astaire, and that when she was tap-dancing, she could click five hundred times per minute. Anyway, the surgeon cut off so much cartilage on one side that the flaw showed up on camera. It was such a disaster the studio makeup department was forced to create a fake nose for filming. During one of her numbers in Cole Porter's **Kiss Me Kate**, she twirled around so fast her nose flew off and hit the camera. I couldn't believe my ears. And as if that wasn't enough, Willie showed Mom and me a photograph of Dean Martin, her hero, before his nose job. "Let's just say it wasn't pretty." That's the way she put it. It wasn't pretty. "And how about this," she said. "Lou Costello, from **The Abbott and Costello Show,** paid for Dean's new nose. That's friendship for you."

I told Willie I didn't believe Dean Martin would do such a thing. Men weren't like women. They didn't care about their looks, did they? She just shook her head and said if I was so smart, why hadn't I heard about Gary Cooper? Didn't I know what had appeared on the front page of the **Mirror-News** a couple of years before? That's right, Gary Cooper's face-lift!

Clearly, I hadn't seen the newspaper article commenting on his face and how it looked "quite different" and how the procedure had "not been successful." The facts were this: fifty-six-year-old Gary Cooper had entered the Manhattan Eye, Ear and Throat Hospital for a full face-lift by Dr. John Converse, one of the leading plastic surgeons in America. Mom and I were baffled. Gary Cooper had a face-lift? Really? But then I thought, Hey, someone had to be the first male movie star to get a face-lift. Why not Gary Cooper? Besides, I identified with the facial dilemmas of Marilyn Monroe, Ann Miller, Dean Martin, and my hero Gary Cooper. Corrections had to be taken seriously.

The bobby pins on my nose, the endless adjustments to my face in search of the right smile at the right angle, the swinging-eye exercises, the celebrity pink lipstick, and the acquired skill of displaying my deepest feelings as if it would improve my countenance were only the beginnings of a determined will to right my wrongs. I'm sorry to say the Corrections didn't do much; nor has their failure stopped me from trying out "solutions" to innumerably more serious "issues," mainly medical. There's my skin cancer regimen, which requires monthly visits to Christie Kidd, who freezes off keratoses, i.e., fledgling skin cancers. There are the endless varieties of creams and lotions, like Renewal Plus, and Solaraze gel, and every imaginable sunscreen. This has made my skin so sunblocked I don't even need to tint the windows of my car. There's the mouth guard worn every night to keep my teeth in place, and the happy brightening gel to make them almost white. I won't go on. The truth is, this is only the beginning of a long list that isn't about beauty; it's about survival.

As far as my face goes, the question is, how far am I willing to go? Particularly at this age. And what would the results give me? With every choice there's a possible gain, but also a loss. I can't say exactly why I haven't turned to surgery or fillers, at least not yet. But what does it matter, particularly now? Why the hell not? Who cares? Maybe I don't want to change my everyday me because I can't picture what I will look like, nor can I imagine what effect it will have on myself or others. I tell myself to hold on to authenticity. But am I authentic? I'll tell you one thing . . . I'm authentically confused by what authentic is. For instance, is it authentic for me to seek out attention by wearing "eccentric" clothes with a lifetime supply of hats? Or is that a look I insist on repeating because it's a habit, a habit that has come to define me? Is it because I admire the unusual? Is it because we're only here once and why not take things as far as you can? Even if it's self-centered, what does it matter—aren't we biologically self-serving animals? Was Georgia O'Keeffe inauthentic and self-consumed when she left Alfred Stieglitz to go live by herself in the desert to paint and pull her hair back and wear Indian jewelry and live her life her way, not the high way? I don't think so. Even if it's narcissistic, is that always such a bad thing? Somebody has to be Joan Rivers, just as somebody has to be Hillary Clinton. Authentic? Inauthentic? I have to laugh. All I know is I'm sick of worrying about my authenticity.

If I want to be prettier, yes, fillers and Botox and a neck-lift would help. I look at my contemporaries who've had "good work." Are they any less authentic? No! And neither are the women who've had procedures that went awry. And yet . . . why haven't I had work done? I still might, though it's borderline too late.

Like most women, I've had some serious disappointments. We each deal with them the best we can. We slather, we dab, we rouge, we nip, we tuck, we ignore, we dream. I don't regret that the face I present to the world is the same I was born with. I've been banged up a bit. I'm older. Actually, I'm a senior citizen. My nose is still my central sense organ. And the bulb? I still hate it, just not as much. I hear with my ears. I eat, speak, and breathe with my mouth. My face includes hair. My forehead is high. I have eyebrows, eyelashes, and two eyes that see. That's my favorite thing about my face. I can see trees and sunsets. I can see Dexter's oval face, and the color of my thirteen-year-old son Duke's eyes: they're chocolate brown, not gray. I can see shadow and light. I can see paintings and portraits on a wall. I can see the ocean from a bluff. I have two ears and two cheeks. With one mouth, one set of lips, one chin, and lots of skin that's still a working vital organ, I'm not complaining. I know from experience how lucky I am. But the most thrilling aspect of my face is its ability to express feelings. All of my feelings and all my emotion come out on my face—my sixty-seven-year-old face. You see, my face identifies who I am inside. It shows feelings I can't put into words. And that is a miracle, an extraordinarily ordinary miracle, one I'll think twice about before I change.

BAD
HAIR DAYS

I woke up knowing this: I had a dream. In my dream I was bald. The rest was unclear. According to **The Dictionary of Dreams,** when a person dreams of hair loss she is concerned with getting older. (No shit.) She is also concerned with losing her sexual appeal. (I'm sixty-seven—what sex appeal?) Approximately thirty minutes later—four forty-five A.M., to be exact—I was sitting shotgun in the Range Rover as my daughter, Dexter, then sixteen years old, began the drive to Oceanside, California, where she would join approximately three hundred people in a 2.4-mile open-water swim in the Pacific Ocean. I pulled down the sun visor and looked in the mirror. No apparent hair loss, at least not for now. Dexter wanted a Carson Daly morning; I wanted to listen to **Morning Edition** with Steve Inskeep and Renée Montagne. We flipped a coin. Dex won. And with it, Carson Daly played Adam Levine's "Payphone." "Yeah, I know it's hard to remember the people we used to be." For sure I couldn't remember the person I used to be, much less the people.

I glanced at Dexter driving south on the 405. She'll never have to worry about a receding hairline. She'll never have hair issues. But I do, and always did. As an underdeveloped, overlooked junior in Santa Ana High School, I was constantly concocting "unique" hairdos, in particular my version of Betty Rubble's "buzzy" beehive. It was just one in a variety of elaborately teased "Big Hairdos" requiring a can of Style hair spray every three days. My inspiration? Dusty Springfield, Cher, and all three of Phil Spector's Ronettes.

Dexter couldn't care less about hair spray. She's a swimmer. I don't understand the kind of mindset that makes a girl walk around with wet hair at six A.M. in the dead of winter, or drench herself in chlorine 250 days a year in swim cap and goggles. When I was young, all girls were forced to wear bathing caps at the public plunge, which made it all the more humiliating when Sawyer Swartz and his gang of geeks would tease me, saying I looked like a jarhead or, worse, a bald-headed Olive Oyl, Popeye's scrawny girlfriend.

The point is, hair, the meaning of hair, the look of hair (my hair, to be exact), has dogged me all my life. Which makes it all the more bizarre that I was cast in the original Broadway production of the musical **Hair**. I remember lying under the scrim one night, waiting to see how many tribe members were going to strip naked, when James Rado, one of the show's creators, stood up with nothing on except a shoulder-length honey-blond wig. I have to say, it was even more riveting than his large penis. His nudity gave the wig a kind of otherworldly glow, a life of its own. Everyone knew Jim was disguising the fact that he was balding. Fine with me. Why not? He was in good company. Sean Connery, Howard Cosell, Burt Reynolds, and Jack Benny wore hairpieces, or toupees, as they called them back then. In any event, no matter how hard James Rado tossed his head back and forth to "give me down to there hair, shoulder length or longer," his wig never swayed, not even an inch.

Once we hit Costa Mesa, Dexter took the Bristol exit in search of gas. As she sped up to make the light, I reminded her that it's best to slow down before approaching an intersection.

My words fell on deaf ears, and Dexter ran her first red light. "It was still yellow before I hit the middle, Mom."

"Listen to me, Dexter. I'll say it again: it's unwise to speed up at an intersection. Okay?! Are you listening to me?"

Silence. I looked over in exasperation and noticed a head of hair so thick it hid her ears. I've never seen her hair part around her ears like mine does. There was a period in the 1980s when I wore a variety of berets to hide my Spock ears because, let's face it, my ears were, and remain, just one more of my many disappointments.

Back to wigs. First there was the one I wore in **The Godfather**. Robert Evans, the head of production at Paramount Pictures, thought I was too "kooky"-looking for the role of Kay Corleone, so Dick Smith, a.k.a. the Godfather of Makeup, turned me into a WASP with a canary-yellow wig ten times larger than my head. Twenty years later I played Bessie, the caregiver sister in **Marvin's Room,** opposite Meryl Streep. Bessie is diagnosed with leukemia, undergoes chemo, and loses all her hair. Throughout most of the two-month shoot, I wore a wig donated from a local candy striper volunteer organization. Jerry Zaks, our director, was enchanted by its authenticity. To me, it was sort of a throwback to Jim Rado's shoulder-length tresses. Only this one was a brunette nightmare from hell. I tried to convince Jerry to give me a chance to wear a hair-hat wig on occasion. Sound strange, a wig sewn into a hat? Not to me. I figured Bessie would look good in a hat. Jerry would have none of it, pointing out that Bessie was not vain. He also added that Bessie was not Diane. Shrugging him off, I continued to press my point, until the day we shot a makeup and hair test for the bald cap I had to wear toward the end of the shoot. As soon as I saw my hairless head, I begged Jerry to please let me keep wearing my candy striper James Rado shoulder-length brown synthetic, almost attractive wig. That is, until the day Meryl told me we both looked like shit. Frankly, I was relieved that she included herself.

The last wig I ever wore, both on- and off-screen, was a curly shag in the practically straight-to-video movie I made with Dax Shepard called **Smother**. Enough said.

As Dexter and I sat in the car at the Chevron gas station, I breathed a sigh of relief. We were two females, one mother, the other daughter. Yes, Dexter had run a red light, but we all make mistakes in the process of learning something new. In the peace of the moment, I mentioned my dream. Dex nodded and, after her quiet way of gathering thoughts, responded with a hair dream of her own: "Okay, Mom, I'm looking through my hair, and it starts falling out in clumps. My head has bloody sores, and blisters, and even holes in the flesh. Every time I look, it's worse than before. It was so creepy. I kept trying to find you and Duke to help. But you were nowhere to be found."

"Wow, Dex, I bet you're glad it's not a reoccurring dream."

"But it is. That's the horrible part, Mom. It is."

I told her that the meaning of dreams is hard to unravel. I told her that she of all people will never have to worry about blisters and sores on her gorgeous hair. Ever. Her hair is perfect. And I was telling the truth.

Woody used to dream of hair loss. Not now. He's done very well retaining what hair he has. Warren used to pontificate on the subject for hours, insisting that hairdressers were worth their weight in gold. According to him, hair was, in fact, 60 percent of good looks. This philosophy must have at least partially inspired him to produce and star in the box office blockbuster **Shampoo**. With hair on his mind, you can imagine how taxing it must have been for him to select the hairstylist for his Oscar-winning movie **Reds**. His pick? Barry Richardson, who did Julie Christie's hair in **McCabe and Mrs. Miller**. Barry was a hairdresser genius, but in truth **Reds** was more hat movie than hair movie. I wore a variety of broad-brimmed hats, several variations on the beret, a number of cloches, and, in one pivotal scene, a peasant scarf tied at the back of my neck. It was all so perfect. I couldn't have been happier. During the weekends I roamed through London's Portobello Road, my favorite flea market. One Sunday, I found a high-crowned black hat with a wide fur trim wrapped around its circumference. I put it on, and, oh yeah, let's just say I bought it on the spot. Later that afternoon, a man with long curlicues dangling on both sides of his face walked past me wearing the identical hat. Shaking his head, he glared at me in an unfriendly manner. When I got back to the hotel, I looked at the label written in Yiddish. Duh. It was what's called a shtreimel. Shtreimel hats are worn exclusively by married male Hasidic Jews, not thirtysomething female actresses. What the hell was I thinking?

And what was I thinking when I tried to seduce Nancy Meyers and Charles Shyer into letting me wear a couple of hats after I was cast opposite Steve Martin in **Father of the Bride**? Nancy reminded me that it was 1991, not 1976. I was playing the mother of the bride, she said, not Annie Hall. During those fifteen years, I let my hair grow halfway to my waist. Nancy let it be known I needed to get a haircut. So I did.

I got back, though. Every day at lunch I would don my bowler hat and join Steve, Marty Short, Kimberly Williams, and Steve's wife at the time, Victoria Tennant, for a plate of spaghetti and some good times. After a couple of weeks Victoria said, "Is every day a bad hair day, Diane?"

I wanted to respond with my own personal philosophy: **Victoria, my hair is my hat. And my hat is my hair.** But of course I said nothing.

Sometimes I wish I was joined at the hip to a great hairstylist like Frida Aradottir or Jill Crosby, who did my hair for the cover of **Ladies' Home Journal**. It's a shame insecurity doesn't bring out my best behavior, but it was a cover, so I felt justified in having a little chat with Jill before the shoot. I began with the bad news. **Ladies' Home Journal** would not, repeat not, let me wear a hat on the cover. I told Jill I was worried about my hair. It needed more volume. I told her that no matter what the editors might say, I wanted it in my face. All of it. I told her the "truth" she already knew in spades: my hair, euphemistically speaking, was unreliable, capricious, erratic, and faithless. I wondered what she could do to help remedy these problems. On cue, Jill got the extensions out of her bag.

As an expert, Jill wanted to set me straight as well. Number 1: if you glue extensions to the top of your head, they will pull off what little hair you have. Number 2: extensions can be seen for the fake hair they are, unless placed in the right location. And Number 3: if you set the extensions as high as possible on either side, it will give the hair on top a better chance to appear full, messy fabulous, and in your face, because as with most things, a foundation is essential.

The cover couldn't have come out better, especially since Brigitte Lacombe, the photographer, doesn't care about hairdos. She cares about the moment. So much so, she may have overlooked the obvious. My left eye was covered by hair, while my right eye was hidden behind blue-tinted glasses. Another bonus of more hair? Less face.

I will say this: the disadvantage of wearing extensions outweighs the advantages. The painful ordeal of removing them takes much longer than putting them in, and they hurt. They really hurt. There are aesthetic problems as well. Extension hair is chunkier, and always superior to the less prevalent, real hair. Plus, the good hair (formerly growing out of someone else's head) won't do what the "bad" hair (mine) insists upon. The whole thing is an endlessly time-consuming folly. Oh, and to make matters worse, it turned out Jill didn't want to be attached to my hip.

At six-thirty Dex parked the Rover in the lot next to the pier where we saw the registration booth. As we walked toward the gathering swimmers, I had the great misfortune to come across my reflection in the window of Johnny Rockets. The news was not good. My hair **is** thinning! And it's not my imagination, nor am I in the middle of a dream I can't remember. It's a fact. I'm losing my hair.

Not to complain, but why me? Why not my sister Dorrie, or my other sister, Robin? Why do all the women in my life have to deliberately flaunt their gorgeous locks? In the beginning it was Mom, with her shoulder-length chestnut-colored hair, which I loved to touch. Then it was Robin, who still has a massive mop. Then Dorrie, whose hair is even thicker than Robin's and more unruly. My business partner, Stephanie, has an ungodly mane. It was the first thing I noticed when I interviewed her for the position, not long after I'd finished filming **Something's Gotta Give**. While she rattled on about her qualifications, all I could think was, Do I really want a brown-haired, brown-eyed junior Cindy Crawford flaunting her blown-out hair in my face five days a week? Do I need to be reminded of my wispy flyaway strands as her fingers shake out her cascading locks, day after day? Forget it. Then I tried to imagine what her hair would look like on my head. One word came to mind:

good. That's what it would have looked like . . .
g-o-o-d.

Then there was Dexter. Sure enough, as she
grew, her hair grew, too. Now it's even more
abundant than Stephanie's. Why do I have to
be surrounded by women whose hair seems to
swish past me as if they're frolicking in a Prell
shampoo commercial? The only relief comes
when they bitch about, I don't know, a bad cut.
Once, Dorrie went temporarily nuts after she
gave herself a Jane Fonda shag trim. I tried not
to enjoy her pain. But come on, give a woman a
break. Goddamnit.

Look, bottom line: I'd like to wish good
thoughts for everyone who's made me feel self-
conscious and miserable about my hair. I'd like
to stop complaining, and stop comparing. I'd
like to be less envious. I'd like to change. I'd
even like to put a smile on my face and be grateful for what I have. All I ask for is this: no disappearing hair follicles, no alopecia, no female
pattern baldness. That's all I want. Nothing more.
That's it.

So, what exactly is hair? I looked it up on my
iPhone while Dexter was getting ready for her
swim. Hair is protein that grows from skin follicles at the rate of about half an inch per month.
Each hair continues to grow for two to six years,

then rests, then falls out. Soon enough, a new hair begins growing in its place. Female pattern baldness occurs when hair falls out and normal new hair does not grow in its place.

Okay? Then there are the signs of impending baldness. What are they? Well, hair thins mainly on the crown of the scalp. It usually starts widening through the center. Symptoms of female pattern baldness include strange hair growth on the face or in the belly button. Another symptom of female pattern baldness can be the enlargement of the clitoris. Does that mean I'm going to have to look at my clitoris to know if I have female pattern baldness? Count me out.

Let's say I am balding. What are some solutions, besides wigs and extensions (which, in reality, can only be used if you actually have hair)? There is transplantation, or plugs, as we used to call them. Dr. Norman Orentreich performed the first transplant surgery in 1952. He coined the term "donor dominance" to explain the basic principles. When hair is relocated, it continues to display the same characteristics of hair from the donor site; in other words, it grows. The downside of Orentreich's technique was that unfortunately, the new hair created an unnatural "corn row" or "doll's hair" look. As I was reading, it dawned on me that I knew Dr. Orentreich. In fact, Woody had used his shampoo to stave off baldness, and it worked. I called the Orentreich Medical Group in New York. A friendly receptionist told me that Norman Orentreich had retired. His son David was running the practice, but unfortunately she was not at liberty to sell me the shampoo since I was not one of his patients. I called Woody, and a week later the shampoo arrived. From Woody Allen, c/o Stephanie Heaton for Diane Keaton. It's been a year since I started using Dr. Orentreich's shampoo. I still have hair, but the jury remains out.

Dexter was now in the ocean, swimming through the surf with a Team Santa Monica bathing cap on her beautiful head. She wasn't worrying about her hair. She was swimming nearly two and a half miles. Imagine that. Amazing. I pulled myself together but not long enough to stop myself from thinking about the only other hair-loss prevention left. Rogaine.

But it turns out that Rogaine can be absorbed through the skin and cause side effects, some of which include unwanted weight gain, hairy face, difficulty breathing, and other symptoms that require calling your doctor. That's when I thought, Oh my God. Forget the labels, the various signs, the definitions, the causes, and the preventions. Face it: every day is a bad hair day and always will be.

The day before the swim, I went to see my

agent, Harvard Law School graduate Nancy Josephson, at her office at the William Morris Endeavor talent agency. I was determined to wear
my hair as a hat, not a hat as my hair. Still, I
wanted to be prepared for the worst, so I tossed
one of my hats in the car. Earlier, I'd looked in
the magnifying mirror and given myself a little
heart-to-heart: "Diane, you're not allowed to
wear the hat today, and here's why: at this point
in your highly privileged life, your hair doesn't
matter to anyone but you. Sorry, but you're fast
becoming a caricature of yourself. How long
do you think you can hide under the brim of a
hat? How long?" I got in the car and turned on
Morning Edition. I was doing just fine, but as
I got closer to WME I started feeling anxious
and pulled over. "Diane, you know what?" I told
myself. "You lack character. There's no validity
to your pronouncements. You are not allowed to
wear the hat to see Nancy Josephson today. Do
you understand? It's final. Your charade is over.
Show a little gumption. It's pathetic. You're sixty-
six years old, and your attitude is not cute."

At Wilshire and Santa Monica, I couldn't take
it any longer, and put the hat on. Wasn't it Randy
Newman who said, "You Can Leave Your Hat
On"? And if Randy said to leave it on, who was
I to disagree? At Wilshire and Camden, I took it
off. At Camden and Brighton, I put it back on.

In the underground parking lot I was so disappointed in myself, I threw the hat in the backseat of the car and told it to go shove itself. Because really, truly, my hair is of no consequence in the scheme of things. DONE!

I left my car with the valet, walked into the elevator, and immediately ran into Nancy. Just my luck. Just my fucking luck. And of course she was chipper and tall and attractive. "You look good," she said. I smiled, knowing she didn't mean it. She hated my hair. When the elevator door opened, I bumped into Adam Venit, one of the agency's partners. Where was my hat when I needed it? Then Maya Forbes, the writer-producer, and her husband, Woody, came over saying, I don't know—something positive about my appearance, I think. But of course I can't remember a compliment, any compliment. It all goes to prove there is no God. But at least I didn't wear the hat, which was getting a much needed break.

Dex was in the water with 299 other people who weren't thinking about their hair. They'd been swimming for fifty minutes so far. Hair was not on their minds, I was reflecting, when I suddenly remembered last night's dream. It all came back as Dexter approached the harbor. . . .

I was flying over a city with lots of churches. The moon was full. Winged people were flying beneath me. I think I was in heaven. I noticed that I had wings too, only mine were black. I asked an angel for a mirror, and screamed when I saw I had no hair. None.

To dream of flying, says **The Dictionary of Dreams,** denotes marital calamities. To dream of flying through the heavens passing the moon foretells famine, wars, and trouble of all kinds. To dream that you have black wings portends bitter disappointments. To dream that you're flying on top of church spires means you will have much to contend against in the way of love, and you will be threatened with a disastrous season of ill health, and, worst of all, the death of someone near to you may follow.

Great! Fine! Forget it. Clearly, there's no relief. I decided to resign myself to baldness, even though I don't really know if I am balding. Yes, my hair is thin, but I can't tell whether I've lost enough to have female pattern baldness; nor am I sure there was a problem to begin with. The glaring possibility is that I may have deluded myself. I am an actress, after all. I still have an active imagination, and I've succeeded in driving myself to distraction, but over what? Thin hair. Not good enough.

After a fifty-eight-minute swim, Dexter came in fourth. She'd overcome five-foot swells in an ocean littered with jellyfish, seaweed, and a few intervening seals. I watched her struggle out of the water and stumble from the shoreline to the finish line. I forgot about my less than seriously big hair, my lifelong struggle, my disappointment and took in the moment, not the future or the past, just the sheer wonder of standing barefoot on a beach watching my daughter receive her fourth-place ribbon. I thought about my own approaching finish line. The way I see hair goes like this:

I have enough to last a lifetime. Dexter has enough to last three lifetimes or more. Our four-and-a-half-hour excursion to Oceanside and back was not meant to be a recap of my hair dilemmas or to compare Dexter's, much less anyone else's, hair with mine. It was not planned to be taken up with envy, the green kind, or wigs, bald caps, hats, and female pattern baldness. But, in my defense, sometimes my mind has a mind of its own.

As I watched Dexter receive her ribbon, her long dirty-blond hair was still wet, still thick, and still perfectly straight. What a beauty, I thought. I had to smile. I couldn't help myself. What a beauty. I felt my smile grow, not just for her but for all the beautiful hair in the world—Mom's chestnut mane, and Dorrie's and Robin's big hair, and Stephanie Heaton's blowout, and Stefanie **Hart to Hart** Powers's as well, and Cybil Shepherd's, plus Zooey Deschanel's, Jessica Alba's, and Caroline Kennedy's untamable mass of hair, in fact all those Kennedy gals', including Maria Shriver's, and what about the endless **Martha Stewart Living** covers, documenting Martha's full head of hair throughout the decades, and Angela Davis's Afro, and even Natalie Portman's shaved head in **V for Vendetta**. How about that for fighting back? What beauties, I thought, each and every one, all and more, in their own way. I had to keep smiling in awe.

THE EYES HAVE IT

If you're like me, always looking for a way to understand how your father played into who you are, warts and all, it makes sense that you'd look to where he spent much of his life. For me and my father, that's the ocean.

I found myself sitting on a bench staring at the Pacific with my old dog Emmie and her friend Speed, a hangdog basset hound, both of whom soon took off after a rabbit. It was eight in the morning. I'd already dropped Duke and Dexter off at the bus stop for school. The ocean spread below me, from the Santa Monica Pier, with its

Ferris wheel dressed up in Halloween lights, all the way up to the edge of Malibu.

During the last years of his life, Dad lived on Cove Street in Corona del Mar, in a three-bedroom oceanfront board-and-batten cottage with his wife of forty-seven years, Dorothy. When he sat on his deck under a Pottery Barn umbrella, he was separated from the ocean by ten feet of concrete decking atop a weathered seawall. I was separated from the water by a sliding cliff. Dad's view of the ocean was in his face. Mine was an all-encompassing panorama below me. Dad and I didn't have too many things in common. Well, that's not true; we did have one thing in common: the shape of our eyes.

Dad never spoke of my eyes, his eyes, or the nature of what eyes see. He spoke **to** me, not **of** me: "Okay, Diane, I want to know what the hell you were thinking when you crashed your mother's Buick station wagon into my work car, which happens to be property of the city of Santa Ana." Or: "Diane"—pause—"if you want to hone your math skills, you need to pay attention, for God's sake." He pontificated on important life lessons like "By failing to prepare, you are preparing to fail." Or: "If you don't know where you're going, how will you know when you get there?" And his ever popular "Diane, I've told you a million times, look before you leap." Staring into Dad's eyes was like going before God. Even when I wasn't in trouble they had a Do Not Enter aspect that kept his vulnerability as far away as the horizon line separating the ocean from the sky.

When I was a little girl, Dad's eyes were blue, bright blue. When I was a big girl, Dad's eyes had plans. They had ambition. They seemed to look to the future for an answer. When I was in my twenties, Dad's eyes sloped down from the weight of various skin cancer extractions. I wondered if living with all those scars had an effect on his relationship to the sun. Mom worried that his blue eyes were fading. He needed sunblock. She asked him to please wear dark glasses. At the beach, he would have none of it. When Dad turned fifty, his eyes seemed to have stretched out like the elastic in an old pair of pajama bottoms. Could it be they were falling from the weight of so many responsibilities?

There was no explanation for their shape. One thing for sure, they didn't come from his mother, Mary, who had prominent lids. Maybe they came from his father, Chester Hall, a barber who was murdered in a union dispute outside Kansas City in the late 1930s. That is, if Chester Hall was in fact Dad's father. When Dad turned sixty, his eyes started drooping so fast they touched his cheeks. I doubt he was happy about it, but he was a man, and men didn't have vanity issues—

at least that's what Dad said. To him, his eyes just were, and that's all there was to it.

Not so long ago I found a snapshot of Dad at age sixty-seven. I compared it with the photograph of me at the same age pinned on Duke's bulletin board. While Dad's eyes look out in truth, mine are hidden behind blue-tinted, black-framed glasses. I'll say this: I've mastered shielding my eyes. But on closer examination, I decided, there was no hiding. Hidden in plain sight was the shape of Dad's eyes in my own. His eyes were playing havoc with my schemes of deception. My eyes are aging exactly like his.

As soon as Emmie returned from chasing the rabbit, I grabbed her muzzle and gave her a big fat kiss. We both looked out over the magnificent horizon. God, is it beautiful here or what? The good news is, our bluff on Asilomar Street offers an unobstructed view of the ocean five blocks wide. There are no $8 million homes blocking the panorama because the bad news is, the earth underneath us continues to move. The most recent landslide sent part of the bluff falling onto the Aloha Courtyard Trailer Park, thirty-five feet below. Beyond the bench I'm sitting on is a sign that says, "Warning! Hazardous Conditions. Do not enter." Dad would have said, "Don't buy near a landslide area. Don't live in the hills. Don't marry a bum." But he was kind enough never to criticize my many attempts to hide the shape of my eyes.

The insults began backstage during a matinee of Woody Allen's Broadway play **Play It Again, Sam.** Our stage manager Mick pulled me aside. "Diane, I hope you don't mind if I ask you something."

"No, go ahead."

"Why do you wear all that black stuff on your eyes? I'd like to see the real Diane. The **Diane** Diane."

Pissed off, I said, "Okay, I get it, you're not into raccoons. Correct me if I'm wrong—weren't you hired to pull the curtain up, not pull actresses aside and give them advice on their appearance? I don't recall asking for beauty tips from Mick, the stage manager. As for all that 'black stuff,' it's none of your business what I do with my eyes. I will tell you one thing: I'm not going to suddenly wake up one morning and see the real Diane, the **Diane** Diane. You know why? Because I am the real Diane. And the real Diane's intention is to flaunt her eyes in smoky blackness for as long as she can."

That's what I wished I'd said. Instead, in typical Diane style, I smiled! I like to blame Dad, who told all us kids early on, "When stuck in a tough situation . . . run." I bet that's not what Chester Hall, the barber, would have done. But then, Dad never knew Chester Hall, who may or may not have been his father. There was no father to help Dad "man up." That was left to Grammy Hall, who was part man anyway. Dad did the best he could. He ran. And so did I. I ran, too.

I ran to Los Angeles as soon as I got a call from my agent telling me the producer of a new Rock Hudson series called **McMillan & Wife** wanted to see me for a role. I was twenty-four years old. The meeting turned out to be a giant lovefest. The producer adored me. He even wanted me to come back for a makeover. The next morning I was ushered into a brightly lit room, where a makeup man named Dan began to scrutinize my face. "We're going to have to do something about those eyes," he said. "They slope. They tell a sad story, not the happy story needed for **McMillan and Wife**." He elaborated on the folds of my eyelids, telling me they hid the natural crease, causing the lower portion of the lid to go unseen. "Okay, I've got it," he said. "I know what to do. Imagine Elizabeth Taylor in **Cleopatra**."

Dan got down to business, applying pale green eye shadow to my disappearing upper lids. He painted wing-tipped curlicues at the ends of my eyes. That's when he said I might want to consider a surgical intervention. He also wanted me to know that he'd deliberately decided not to use black eye pencil inside the bottom lids because, frankly speaking, it was "aging," especially considering my "Asian eyes." After what seemed an interminably long time, he finished with a flair and gave me the hand mirror. When I looked at twenty-four-year-old Diane Hall from Orange County who went to New York City to become an actress, hopefully in the movies, that Diane, the one I'd grown up with, was gone.

"Huh, Dan, can I speak to you for a moment? Look, I know it was a horrible shame the door opened and there was dreary-eyed Little Miss Me. Sorry about that. Granted, it was unfortunate you were stuck with a pair of 'hooded eyes' only a mother could love. But did you really have to turn me into a wide-eyed Kewpie doll? Painting swirly tails at the ends of my eyes is not going to make me Cleopatra, and why Cleopatra in the first place? Here's what kills me. Here's what I can't get over. I looked pretty enough to win the honor of a makeover. I just wasn't pretty enough to avoid you. And, by the way, with all due respect, I'm twenty-four years old, not forty-four, the new twenty-four. I actually am twenty-four. So don't tell me eyeliner is aging, 'cause unlike you, I'm too young to be aging. I know there's no chance in hell I'm going to make the cut. But guess what, Dan the makeup man, you will not have the opportunity to chime in because . . . I'm out of here, you big jerk."

That's what I wanted to say. Instead, I sat in the producer's office with Dan as the producer oohed and aahed over my transformation before escorting me out the door. The next day I got the call from my agent saying they loved me, but they were going in a different direction. The Susan Saint James direction, to be exact.

Suddenly Speed joined Emmie in barking at Prince, the Great Dane, who loped off in his version of a run and knocked over the warning sign. I had to laugh. If only Dad could sit with me one time before the bench slides into the trailer park below. If he were here, I could open the conversation with something harmless, like how funny Speed's ears look dragging through the dirt, or wasn't it a shame it took so long to wax our Hobie surfboards back in the day, and what ever happened to **Boomerang,** our first speedboat. That might be nice. I'd be sure to leave out the summer I got burned in another way: the summer I saw my first penis. I say "burned" because after that initial "glimpse," like in the Alicia Keys song, this girl was on fire. All I did was walk into our tent and there was Dad's friend Jim, with his organ exposed. It happened so fast I couldn't take in the details. I wanted to, but despite the current unpopularity of Sigmund Freud and his even less popular theory of penis envy, I have to say the power of his penis struck an envious note in me. Even though I've had some long, hard looks inside Taschen's **The Big Penis Book,** the picture of Jim changing out of his swim trunks looms, like Goya's black landscapes engorged with screaming monsters, hell, fire, and damnation. For me, the penis will always be a source of wonder, and fear. But, of course, Dad and I could never talk of such things, partially because he had one, partially because he was my father, but mainly because it was a risky conversation for two people who didn't know how to speak to each other even though we shared a pair of identically shaped eyes.

Our love didn't include hugs and kisses, and I remember only a few times when I held his hand like other girls did with their fathers. This made our eyes—not what we saw, or how we engaged the world, but the concrete, undeniable shape of our eyes—all the more meaningful. Like I said, it makes sense that if I'm looking for a way to understand how my father played into who I am, of course I'd find myself sitting on a bench twenty-three years after his death, trying to see beyond the blue of the ocean into the once living blue of my father's eyes. It's a risk worth taking. And I take it every day. Even if I'm distracted.

I never fail to think of the boy who loved the ocean, the boy who grew up to be the man with the house sitting on the edge of the continent. Sometimes I imagine combining Dad's eyes with mine. Together they'd slide so far down the hill they'd touch the ocean below. Only he and I, and maybe hangdog Speed, know the joy of the rise before the beauty of the fall.

Dad must have spent fifteen years of his life looking at the largest body of water on earth. I think of all the times he dove off the cliffs of Palos Verdes and Divers Cove. I think of him stretching his feet against the sand on Rincon and Dana Point and Zuma Beach and Topanga, too. I think of him surfing at Salt Creek Beach, and camping at Doheny State Beach. I think of the sound our Buick station wagon made as he drove across the train tracks to San Clemente. I think of the chair he sat in at the old house across the bay from the Balboa Fun Zone, in Newport Beach. I think of that same chair with Dad in it, at his new house, the last house, the house overlooking the mouth of the bay at the tip of Corona del Mar. Where did it go?

Dad didn't leave a record of what he saw, or the way he saw it. Yet nearly one-quarter of his life was given to the art of looking. All those grabbed hours, those sunburned moments collected over a lifetime of observations shared with no one but himself. He must have known that the ritual would disappear when he did.

Sometimes, to help kick-start one of our imaginary conversations, I play back our one milestone memory. I've told it before, but it's the only one I have. It was 1963. The curtain had fallen on Santa Ana High School's production of **Little Mary Sunshine.** My rendition of Nancy Twinkle's "Mata Hari," a song about a spy who brought men to their knees by "doing this and that-a" had just given me the only standing ovation of my life. On the way to change out of my costume I saw Dad approach from backstage. He stopped in front of the red velvet curtain, stepped in close, and looked me straight in the eyes for what seemed like an eternity. He did not speak, yet his face, lit by the blue of his eyes, told me a story. It was not the story of a father who repeatedly reminded his daughter to plan ahead and use her noggin. All plans had been temporarily canceled. This father's face paled from the glow reflected in his eyes. This father told the story of a daughter who, against all odds, had suddenly landed on the sacred ground of "right," even though her "right" was a multitude of "wrongs." She would put these wrongs to good use in a venue she would continue to pursue for the rest of her life. Performing. It would be the only time I would see my father's face beam with pride for the very wrongs that made me right; by this I mean my endless tears, the vague distractions, the awkward hesitancy, and my annoying brand of being "so sensitive that you're insensitive." Just like the standing ovation, it was the first and only time Dad looked at me with unabashed joy.

I'm still trying to convince myself that the identical shape of our eyes must mean we were not opposites. We must have shared feelings and dreams and fears, too. We must have. It's true I collect objects of beauty, like John Stezaker's collages, while Dad collected jars full of nickels and dimes. I love the G-Wagen. Dad was consumed by the gas he saved with his Toyota 4Runner. Dad thought function was beauty, not form. I choose form over function every time. On the functioning front, Dad tried to make me do things right, like "plan ahead" and "look before you leap." But there was always something wrong interfering. That is, until **Little Mary Sunshine**. Dad didn't write his thoughts down the way Mom did. There is no evidence. My investigation into our similarities is nothing more than conjecture. All that's left is the ocean he stared at, and our tumbling eyes. It doesn't give me much to go on.

"Dad, can I ask you something from the other side of the great mystery? How much of what you saw is what I see? It might sound crazy, but sometimes I believe I'm seeing things from inside your eyes. Am I? I wish. In three short months I will be the same age as you were when you died. I can still see the smoky blue tint of your eyes. I can still see the red velvet curtain, and the crowds parting almost as if I were Maria in **West Side Story,** to your Tony. Here on the bluff, looking at the ocean, I wish I could share with you a truth I've come to believe: It's all in the eyes. Our eyes. Yours. And mine."

TURTLENECKS AND TIES, BIKINIS AND BRAS

I've never known a woman who didn't love to shop. My sister Robin is a Ross Dress for Less maven. Dorrie, my baby sister, loves North Face and Tommy Hilfiger. My friend Susie Becker is a walking dictionary of fashion, with a closet the size of a costume rental store. Carol Kane loves sacky dresses in prints à la Marni and Yohji Yamamoto. All my girlfriends love to shop. Then there's my daughter, Dexter. She is not a shopper.

I named Dexter after Cary Grant's character in **The Philadelphia Story**, C. K. Dexter Haven. She arrived in a basket eight days into life wearing a pink ruffled dress with a white bib trimmed in red. I was ready for action. Off with the fussy garb and on with a pair of black leggings, matching cap, licorice loafers, and ebony socks. Dexter was among the first to have a Baby Gap wardrobe of gray striped onesies accessorized with plaid bibs, Vans slip-ons, and a Billabong baby trucker hat. For her first Christmas I bought her a hound's-tooth baby boy suit and a pair of vintage cowboy boots I found at the Long Beach swap meet. My reign of terror ended when she was able to distinguish pink and purple from black and gray. As soon as she could string a couple of sentences together, Dexter let me know she didn't take to boys' trousers and she wasn't going to be a princess in black. She was her own Dexter, and she was living in color.

By the time I turned fifteen, I was my own Diane, and I was living in Black and White. It began after the annual family trip to Grauman's Chinese Theatre, on Hollywood Boulevard, where we saw **The Wizard of Oz.** I was so upset I wrote Judy Garland and asked her to explain why Dorothy had to leave Kansas for Oz. She didn't write back. But when I saw Cary Grant as C. K. Dexter Haven in **The Philadelphia Story,** I couldn't believe my eyes. I was so excited I wrote to him, asking for an autographed eight-by-ten glossy. Two weeks later, a manila envelope arrived with a picture of him wearing thick-rimmed glasses that offset his dark eyes, his square jaw, and that dazzling smile. I didn't want a picture of Katharine Hepburn, his costar, who I thought of as upper-crust. Plus, I didn't cotton to her long gowns or shoulder-padded suits with A-shaped skirts. In fact, I felt sorry for her, and could never have dreamed that one day she would be one of my heroes. She probably had to wear corsets every day in order to have an hourglass figure. Big deal. The last thing I wanted was to be hemmed in by a twenty-one-inch waist. Katharine Hepburn must have been terribly uncomfortable. Maybe that's why she stomped around the Lord family mansion with a snooty sense of entitlement, while Cary Grant skipped through the stuffy atmosphere in double-breasted pin-striped suits with black loafers and white socks. He wore things like white cardigan sweaters thrown ever so casually over his shoulders after a game of tennis, or a tuxedo with a white bow tie for afternoon tea, just for the fun of it, "old man."

My "Things and Stuff" scrapbook was crammed with pictures of him in turtleneck sweaters under crisp striped shirts, and herringbone jackets over tweed pants. He wasn't afraid of a polka-dot tie or handkerchief. He wore gray worsted wool suits with wide lapels, a waist button, a white shirt, and his collar up. I also wrote down several of Mr. Grant's fashion tips. For example, he knew that the proper look of a tie lies in a taut knot. If not executed to perfection, the knot loses the necessary spring to arch out from the collar. He believed every man should own a variety of ties, adding that he preferred the relatively wide sort while never venturing near what might be considered "over the top." I wrote down two of his famous quotes. Number 1: "Clothes make the man." And Number 2: "I pretended to be somebody I wanted to be, and I finally became that person." I had no doubt I could be the person I wanted to be if I applied Cary Grant's concept that "clothes make the man"—or, in my case, "clothes make the woman."

When Dexter turned fifteen, she received a two-hundred-dollar gift card to Victoria's Secret. I had to drag her into their store on the Third Street Promenade in Santa Monica, where we were welcomed by aisles of boy shorts with messages like "Life of the Party" and "Unwrap Me" printed on the crotch. We passed hipster panties spelling out "No Peeking" and "Let's Go Skinny Dipping" on the butt. At the million-dollar Fantasy Bra display, Dexter informed me she'd recently become a C cup. Wait a minute, a C? When did that happen? Just yesterday she was a solid B. Was she going to become one of those breast-implant gals who fears she'll never be big enough? Surely she didn't want to become an oversized Dexter cow with a couple of udders dragging on the floor? Dex kept insisting she was a C cup. I kept insisting she was a B . . . and that was it. End of discussion. She marched off to find a saleslady.

Left alone, I couldn't get over the evolution of underwear at Victoria's Secret. Everything was so friendly. Except for those few years in the early 1970s when I didn't wear one, I'd never thought of bras as anything but a necessity one had to address. Occasionally I come across pictures of myself from the braless days. What the hell was I doing? Soooo unattractive. And my poor little breasts. They must have been confused. At a party recently I reminisced with my old friend Elliott Gould, who said, "Oh, I remember you from the seventies—you had those low-slung tits." Several years ago, I was about to make a movie called **Because I Said So** when the costume designer, Shay Cunliffe, wanted to know if I had any favorite bras she might borrow in case she needed to buy extras. I brought in several standbys from when I'd filmed **The First Wives**

Club, a decade earlier. Trying to hide her shock, Shay gently informed me that most women toss their bras after a year.

When Dexter came back with a saleslady named Jane, she was all fired up. Suddenly she wanted four bras and a dozen panties. This was definitely a new Dex. Passing what seemed to be thousands upon thousands of sexy boy-short panties and padded, leopard-skin bras encrusted in pink rhinestones, Jane walked us to the dressing rooms painted, you got it, pink. A stock boy almost knocked me down as he flew past with several boxes of undies to put on display. I couldn't help but wonder what kind of fantasies played havoc in his mind as he placed "Santa's Helper" ruched panties in drawers under display bins with "Eat Me," "Come Here Often?" and "69" printed on a veritable universe of crotches.

Unaffected, Jane measured Dexter for her cup size, taking note of her broad back. Was Dexter a swimmer? she inquired. Dexter nodded. And yes, Jane agreed, it appeared Dexter's cup size was a C. She suggested that when in doubt Dexter might want to try both the C cup and the B. Now, that's an expert for you. With that taken care of, she handed Dexter what could only be described as bras on a stick in every imaginable shape and style. Reassured, Dexter shut the door, while I checked out the vibe at Victoria's. This is

what I saw: I saw a family of women from vary-
ing walks of life loving their underwear. I wished
sex was as harmless and free-spirited as the atmosphere in Victoria's Secret. Not to cast asper-
sions, but there are women like Jodi Arias and
Jean Harris for whom sex goes awry. But here in
benign Victoria's Secret, it's easy to forget that
sex is capable of bringing out such murderous
rage. Speaking of Victoria, I wonder if there is an
actual Victoria. If so, I'd like to meet her some-
time and have a serious chat about her "Eat Me"
underwear. All in the name of good fun, mind
you.

Shame permeated the ambience in the bra department of Newberry's five-and-ten-cent store in
Santa Ana, where I worked as a salesgirl in 1960.
Bras were embarrassing, dreary things; certainly
not fun. There were no colors. Each style sat in
ugly plastic boxes, in aisle after aisle filled with
other ugly plastic boxes. Women didn't come to
Newberry's expecting a private dressing room
with a lovely Jane-type saleswoman carrying
her ever ready measuring tape while dispensing
sage advice. No way. Buying a bra was like buying Kotex. The unattended cotton Maidenform
bras had names like "Snoozable" and "Sweet
Dreams." Hardly dangerous, and hardly sexy.
After hours of folding them neatly before placing them into containers, I felt nothing if not

embarrassed, but also secretly curious. One day I got caught red-handed placing a 32B padded Wonderbra over my sweater to see what it would look like. Oh my God, you'd think I'd committed a crime. Mr. Olsen, the assistant manager, immediately downgraded me to a cash register in the hardware department. He didn't understand. I'd been compelled to feel the cushioned fabric that made one's breasts a Wonder.

According to my friend Leona Cramer, if you dared to wear a Wonderbra you not only became a girl who has intercourse with boys, gets pregnant, and has a baby, but you also became a liar for life. As much as I told myself I was not the kind of girl who would ever buy a padded bra, I did. Just once. I did. I snuck over to Penney's department store, where I purchased the oh-so-evil Wonderbra and wore it to school the next day. At lunch, my longtime crush Dave Garland poked his finger into the left 32B cup, where it stuck like glue to my flat chest. Mortified, I ran home, promising myself I would never lie again.

Meanwhile, in Victoria's Secret I was surrounded by a lot of happy women enjoying the fun of being sexy. The experience was downright wholesome. I was beginning to feel like Victoria had invited me to her colorful, lighthearted home. After a while, Jane breezed down the hallway and knocked on Dexter's dressing room door. Dex peeked out and showed Jane how she looked in the 34C bra. Jane took a long, hard look at Dexter's breasts and nodded yes to the 34C. Perfect. The next step? Bra style. Dex lined up three favorites. Pink's Heartbreaker Push-Up Plunge Bra. Pink's Wear Everywhere Lightly Lined Bra. And her favorite, Pink's Campus Push-Up Bra. Thrilled though she was, Jane also suggested that Dexter might include Pink's Yoga Push-Up Bra with Mesh, a more natural every-day, after-swimming sports bra. Dexter nodded her head.

Victoria's marketing genius was simple: she gave women the right to choose their own un-derwear. No more waiting for husbands and lov-ers to buy that Valentine's Day black lace garter belt or a see-through push-up bra with little holes for the nipples from Frederick's of Hollywood. Those days are over. Women can choose their own "sexy lady" underwear. Dexter placed the gift card on the checkout counter. She put down her four Pink bras, three Pink Cheekster panties, three Pink thongs, and three Pink Cheekini boy shorts. She was a happy, newly fledged moder-ate shopper. I was excited for Dexter, and grate-ful to Victoria for letting a girl be a girl—but mainly for giving sex a lighter spin. Nevertheless, the world in Pink was beginning to wear thin. I was ready to go home to Black and White and

Gray all over. I wanted to be light on my feet, like Cary Grant. I wanted to put on a smoky gray dress suit with suspenders. I wanted to be an international stilt walker, with an ironic smile and a dimpled chin.

If, like Dexter's, your body is voluptuous; if it curves in wondrous ways; if you have broad shoulders and a broad back; if you have killer hips and a round bottom that's hard as a rock; if you're all woman and you love your body like Dexter does hers, Victoria's Secret is a safe fun-house haven. But if your favorite word when you were little was "tomboy" and if you ran to the arroyo to climb trees and pretend you were Davy Crockett, king of the wild frontier, in a coonskin cap, then where the hell do you shop when you're a grown-up looking for a little fun with the menswear look? Where's the equivalent of Victoria's Secret, complete with merchandise like "Life of the Party" boxer shorts written on a different kind of crotch? Where's the shop for those of us who want to play around with part-time gender bending?

All in all, just about every female celebrity has dabbled in men's clothes, even if only for a photo shoot. Think Marlene Dietrich cross-dressing in a man's tux. Think Amelia Earhart in pullover sweaters and khakis. Think Ellen DeGeneres in a vest with a casual white shirt underneath and a pair of Paige jeans and white tennis shoes. Come on, where's that store? And what's it called? How about "Ellen's Crossing"? I'd shop there. Who wouldn't? I promise you it'd be just as mind-expanding and fun as Victoria's Secret, even for the accessories alone—the hats, the fingerless gloves, the turtlenecks, the socks, the shoes, the scarves. Come on, Ellen loves a scarf now and then. Why doesn't every city have an "Ellen's Crossing" with its own delicious secret? Victoria had one.

I always thought feminine meant delicate, frightened, and helpless. Because of Cary Grant's allure, and the thought of dancing through life in black and white, I've always been drawn to men's clothes. Now that I'm sixty-seven, I'm aware that fear is not gender-based. You could call a good two-thirds of my wardrobe an impenetrable fortress. By this I mean the hats that hide the head, the gloves that hide the fingers, the long-sleeved turtlenecks that hide both the arms and the neck, the leggings that hide the legs, and the boots that hide the feet.

Let's take the turtleneck. Turtlenecks are particularly underrated. Buy one. I dare you. Give one a try. Turtlenecks cushion, shield, and insulate a person from harm. Never let a turtleneck's collar sag. Get smart and sew stays at both side seams. It will keep your turtleneck gravity-free.

Make sure the fabric isn't too bulky, unless you want a linebacker's neck. If you take my advice, trust me, your head will be framed to perfection. Buy one. Be brave. If it turns out that you begin to wear turtlenecks as often as I do, and you're my age, and you're not Cary Grant, you will run the risk of receiving a fair amount of criticism. Even though turtlenecks worked well for my costumes in **Something's Gotta Give,** there was an implied criticism when Harry Sanborn, played by Jack Nicholson, says, "I just have one question: What's with the turtlenecks? I mean, it's the middle of summer." Erica, played by me, replies, "Well, I guess I'm just a turtleneck kind of gal." Harry: "You never get hot?" Erica: "No." Harry: "Never?" Erica: "Not lately." And it's true, I never get hot.

At this point, no one criticizes Dexter's choice of Pink underwear. She's not a Victoria's Secret model. She isn't wearing her "Let's Party" Pink boy shorts on display. Online recently, I saw a paparazzi picture of myself under the headline "Diane Keaton and Her Daughter." We were on the streets of Beverly Hills. It was a study in contrasts. She had on a pair of Old Navy USC red Trojan shorts, flip-flops, and a pale blue H&M sweatshirt with iPod wires sticking out of her ears. True to form, I was duded out in black leather platform boots, gray-and-black plaid ski pants, a black Uniqlo Jil Sander coat with a four-inch-wide belt cinched in at my waist, a white shirt, polka-dot gloves, and the ever present wide-brimmed hat. It was seventy-eight degrees outside. I did not look like Cary Grant, and Dexter did not look like Stephanie Seymour. We looked like the yin and yang of life, Frick and Frack, the Odd Couple. No one would assume we were mother and daughter. Not only was the age difference working against us, but so was the choice of how we present ourselves to the world. That was the truth as documented in a paparazzi photograph posted online. Underneath the photograph was this comment: "Actress Diane Keaton stepped out wearing yet another one of her Annie Hall–inspired ensembles to go Christmas shopping in Beverly Hills. However as the 65-year-old confidently strutted ahead, her young daughter Dexter trailed behind, possibly in embarrassment." What the photographer did not capture, and what the commenter missed, was this: under Dexter's casual running shorts and hooded sweatshirt was the exuberant world of a private imagination at play.

As for shopping? Think Big. Think Small. Think Different. Beauty Outside. Beast Inside. American by Birth. Rebel by Choice. Make the Most of Now. Because You're Worth It. When the World Zigs, Zag. Decry Complacency. Think

Outside the Bun. Have It Your Way. Just Do It. If You've Got It, Flaunt It. Does She Or Doesn't She? The United Colors of Benetton. We're not liberal America or conservative America—we're part of the United States of America. You're you. I'm me. And Dexter's Dexter. It's just as okay to be the old flamboyant as it is to be the young casual. It's great to be the mind behind J. Crew and Ralph Lauren, and Quiksilver, and H&M. It's fantastic to have an imagination stimulated by diversity. It's a world of style influenced by Coco Chanel and Miuccia Prada and Paul Harnden, too. It's Rihanna and Beyoncé and Nicki Minaj. It was thrift-store Barbra Streisand in the 1970s and Madonna's street-smart layered look of the '80s. It was Romeo Gigli in the '90s. Now it's Paul Smith's classic schoolgirl look and Thom Browne's **Mad Men** suits. It's Anna Wintour's hatred of Black teamed up with Grace Coddington's love of Orange. It's the Row, by Mary-Kate and Ashley Olsen. It's Louis Vuitton designed by Marc Jacobs. For me? It's Cary Grant and Dexter Keaton. It's women in men's clothes made for women. It's Bill Cunningham on his bicycle shooting the fashion trends of men and women on the streets of New York City. It's Victoria's Secret and Ellen's Crossing. It's potential for change, and it's change itself. It's turtlenecks and ties, and bikinis and bras.

WHAT IS BEAUTY?

This morning the ocean was beautiful. But what does that even mean? Cloudy with pockets of blue? Hazy gray, hardly a blue kind of blue? Blue peppered with pale pink? Suddenly those hazy gray clouds parted and from the bluff I could see two ships spotlit by the sun. Was that beauty?

That's what I was thinking when it dawned on me my sister Robin still hadn't called me back. She'd been crying about her dog Dash's penchant for attacking her next-door neighbor's awful Chihuahua, Joanie, when Dylan, her four-year-old grandson, started screaming. She said she'd call me right back and hung up. But she hadn't. So, was the ocean beautiful this morning? Or was it background music for my agitation? Mom had loved describing flawless beauty, especially in her journals. She never dirtied it up with doubts. But beauty isn't perfect. And neither is Robin, who still hasn't called me back. What the hell is beauty?

I was a stubborn girl. I remember cutting a deal with Mom, saying I'd learn to read but only if the books were illustrated with pictures. Wasn't it Alice in Wonderland who peeked into the pictureless book her sister was reading and said to herself, "What is the use of a book without pictures?" In the Dick and Jane series, co-authors William S. Gray and, Zerna Sharp wrote, "Oh, see. Oh, see Jane. Funny, funny Jane." I saw Jane because she was illustrated. Years later, I saw Keith Carter's portrait of a black dog because Keith Carter took the photograph. Reading is seeing, too. But it requires more thought. Is thought beautiful? Some thoughts are. So what is beauty? For me, it's a collection of images, and objects, and thoughts, and feelings I've gathered over the course of my life. Dad would have numbered beauty. Mom wrote it down. Dexter listens to it. Duke wants to own it, all of it, in every shape and form. Sometimes beauty, like today, is a closed book I can't open. Sometimes it's hanging in my closet. Like my dad's old sweater. Sometimes it's a message saved on my voice mail. . . . But one thing for sure: all of it is personal.

LOST DOG BY KEITH CARTER

Several years ago my old dog Josie had lost her appetite. At the vet's, Dr. Kalin drew blood, took X-rays, and listened to her heartbeat. A week later, the call came. Josie's liver count was high. Cushing's disease was mentioned. Even though Jaws—that's what I called her after she bit the mailman—was a nasty shepherd mix, I loved her. Fifteen years after she passed, I saw her essence in Keith Carter's portrait called **Lost Dog**. His dog is black, and maybe not so old, but in that face, with its predominant nose much too close to the camera lens; in his blurry, soulful gaze; in his loyalty, his sweet trust, I saw Josie. I saw our twelve years together. I saw my dread of losing her. I saw that her loss has been a sadness I will carry with me all the days of my life.

Josie, my Jaws, had been reawakened in a photograph taken by a man I didn't know. The subject was a dog I'd never seen. Keith Carter wrote this: "For me, a portrait is something that has a certain weight, a certain seriousness to it. . . . These days, I treat everything as a portrait, whether it's a safety pin hanging from a string in a woman's bedroom, or a man witching for water in a field. They're the same. They are all equal, I try to give them the same weight."

WENDY, THE MADAME ALEXANDER DOLL

One day Mom drove me to my friend Mary Lou's house. It was on the other side of the 110 freeway. That meant one thing: her house would be shabby and small. When our station wagon pulled up I saw I wasn't wrong, and the inside was no better. Off the narrow hallway were four doors. Behind door number 3 was Mary Lou's bedroom. When she opened it, I was struck dumb. There on a bookshelf as big as the wall stood a museum-sized collection of Madame Alexander dolls. Nine-year-old-me wasn't prepared for a feeling I'd never had before. I'll say this: it wasn't good. Why did Mary Lou's parents, who lived on the other side of the 110, have enough money to buy her hundreds of the most collectible doll ever? Why hadn't Mom and Dad given me the Scarlett O'Hara doll for Christmas, or at least one of the famous Dionne quintuplet baby dolls from 1936, and the Queen Elizabeth the Second doll, too? But the worst possible shock, the one I wasn't able to handle with even a modicum of grace, was Mary Lou's brand-new eight-inch Wendy, the bridesmaid doll, in a pink ruffled gown, with a perfect straw hat balanced on top of her curly blond hair.

One week later, I was called into my parents' bedroom. Mary Lou's mother, Nancy, had phoned our house on the party line, wanting to know if I'd unintentionally taken the Madame Alexander Wendy doll. That's when I understood that beauty could be evil. It could make a perfectly good girl like me turn into the devil. So, what is beauty? When I was nine, it belonged to someone else, and I made it MINE, consequences or not.

THE LEGACY OF BILL WOODS, JR.; OR, THE FAMILY OF MAN

Bill Woods, Jr., was a professional photographer who documented life in Fort Worth for several decades after World War II. His studio on Hawkins Street was a hub of activity. He drove a yellow VW Bug. He wore bow ties. He took a picture of an adolescent girl in a bathing suit with a football-sized tumor protruding from her thigh. He took a picture of Eleanor Roosevelt shaking hands with a man in front of a curtain. He took a picture of a man holding a rifle standing next to a dead bear hanging by its feet. He took a picture of two nuns seated in a bare room with a small TV in the corner and a black man in a janitor's uniform cleaning a white porcelain bowl. I bought every one of the twenty thousand photographs Bill Woods, Jr., took with his large-format camera.

Bill Woods's photographs were commissioned by a variety of local patrons, who posed in front of a series of backdrops culled from real life. But reality vanished with the click of Mr. Woods's camera. Diane Arbus said, "For me the subject of the picture is always more important than the picture. And more complicated." That was the result, if not the intention, of Bill Woods's life work. His subjects were, as Diane Arbus said, more complicated than the story each photograph was trying to tell.

Bill Woods was no Diane Arbus. Bill Woods got the job done. He recorded life in Fort Worth. He gave his clients validation, just not the way they expected. Bill Woods's work is a reminder that none of us are that much different from the folks of Fort Worth. We all long to feel confident, look great, and do well. We all want to be remembered. Sometimes we're lost. Sometimes we're found. But one thing's for sure: no matter how much control we have over our appearance, we're all awkward, laughable, ugly, and beautiful at the same time. The only difference between Bill Woods's patrons and me is this: my life has been documented by more than one photographer. Like others, to the best of my ability I've tried to create a Diane Keaton I want the future to see.

A SNAPSHOT OF DOROTHY HALL LAUGHING

I woke up in the middle of the night five hours after my mother's body, draped in a purple cloth, had been wheeled out of the kitchen on a gurney. I woke up knowing there would never be another person to replace her. I would have to rely on myself. I knew that the days of little high-foreheaded Di-annie Oh Hall-ie had been wheeled away with Dorothy.

Life keeps moving forward, as if following a predictable time line. I was a girl, I grew up, I became an adult, I reached middle age, I worked hard to accomplish my goals, I got old, I watched people die, and I said my goodbyes, including farewells to a couple of sparrows who flew into my plate-glass window unaware. I've had a life, and soon it will be reasonable to expect me to let it go with grace. But that's not the way it works for some of us.

Like the sparrows, I've flown into some serious plate-glass windows, but I survived. On the way, I've learned a few things. Namely this: beauty's a bouquet gathered in loss. The sad part about my bouquet is that it keeps growing. Now that

Mother is gone, darkness is spreading across my fading petals. Light is beautiful, but darkness is eternal.

I live with the beauty of regret, and the memory of love. I feel it when I feed cheddar cheese to Dexter's rats, Ludicrous and Nala. I watch them hold the orange strips in their almost human hands as they trim the cheese with delicate precision. I see Mother's hands. I see her fingers throwing bread crumbs to the pelicans on the seawall. I believed in Mother's permanence. I believed in the radiance of her face in the photograph Dad took of her with her head thrown back in laughter. When I try to make her photograph laugh in three dimensions, I feel the sorrow of beauty lost.

BERENICE ABBOTT'S **PARABOLIC MIRROR,** THE MIRROR WITH A THOUSAND EYES

There's "a bird's-eye view," "a gleam in the eye," and "a roving eye." There's "a sight for sore eyes" and "a worm's-eye view," too. Don't forget "all eyes are on you"—that's a favorite. Or "an eye for an eye" or "don't bat an eye" or, especially, "be in the eye of the storm." I love "bedroom eyes" and "I can't take my eyes off of you," but I don't want "a black eye." I'd give anything to be "eye candy" and "more than meets the eye." There's always the old standby "Don't try to pull the wool over my eyes." As far as I'm concerned, I don't want to take the "red-eye," even if "we're seeing eye to eye." If you want to, try to get some "shut-eye," then don't let the "stars get in your eyes," because you're the "apple of my eye." And never "turn a blind eye," "without batting an eye," especially with "your eyes wide open." In the end, "there wasn't a dry eye in the house," because "beauty is in the eye of the beholder."

WORDS FROM MORRIS FRIEDELL (VIA DAVID SHENK'S **THE FORGETTING**)

"I fantasized about being an 'astrogator.' We collide with an asteroid; there is not enough fuel to get back to earth. We turn the ship straight away from the sun, we voyage out beyond the orbit of Pluto. We know we will perish in the interstellar void, yet we hope to radio back to earth images of beauty never seen as well as valuable information. . . . On August 19, 1998, my neurologist told me [Alzheimer's] is what the PET scan indicated. And here I am on that spaceship. . . . I find myself more visually sensitive. Everything seems richer: lines, planes, contrast. It is a wonderful compensation. . . . We [who have Alzheimer's disease] can appreciate clouds, leaves, flowers as we never did before. . . . As the poet Theodore

Roethke put it, 'In a dark time the eye begins to see.'"

SILVER LININGS PLAYBOOK

I was with my friend Diane English at the Landmark theater on Pico. We were eating popcorn and watching **Silver Linings Playbook.** The setup went like this: Bradley Cooper is locked up in a mental institution. He's bipolar. That means he has no control over his impulses. He wants his wife back. One day his mother gets him out. They drive home. He runs into a friend. The friend invites him over for dinner. Bradley Cooper meets Jennifer Lawrence. They lock eyes.

That's when the movie stopped cold. That's when my heart went into my throat. Bradley Cooper says, "You look nice." Jennifer Lawrence says, "Thank you." Bradley Cooper pauses, then says, "I'm not flirting with you." Jennifer Lawrence says, "Oh, I didn't think you were." Bradley Cooper says, "I just see that you made an effort and I'm gonna be better with my wife, I'm working on that. I wanna acknowledge her beauty. I never used to do that. I do that now. 'Cause we're gonna be better than ever." It was like the line Montgomery Clift said to Elizabeth Taylor in **A Place in the Sun:** "I love you. I've loved you since the first moment I saw you. I guess maybe I've even loved you before I saw you."

That was the subtext. That was the moment. It was like Renée Zellwegger when she said "shut up" to Tom Cruise in **Jerry Maguire:** "Just shut up. You had me at 'hello.'" It was better than every great kiss I'd ever seen or been given. It was flawed beauty. Fucked-up beauty. It was bigger and better than life. It was art. It was sex, and it was love. Bradley and Jennifer didn't know it, but that was the moment we became a threesome. Even now, months later, I can close my eyes and look into Bradley's eyes knowing he's seeing me and Jennifer. I look into Jennifer's eyes and know she's seeing his and mine. I know what he's hiding. I know what she's afraid of. . . . I own their comings and goings. I'm the third wheel of a beautiful moment on film. And it's all in my head.

A PHOTOGRAPH OF DUKE

His curly blond hair is suddenly brown. His angelic baby face is adolescent. He still hugs me. I'm still his Cheeks. But the most remarkable thing is . . . no matter how much Duke hates my nagging about his homework ("More detail, Duke"), no matter how much he screams when I tell him we're watching the documentary **Poor Kids** on PBS instead of **Jersey Shore,** from which he's memorized quotes like "Get your weiner cleaner" and "Work blows shit for Skittles," no matter how much I harp on eating more avocado, and greens, and his oatmeal with almonds, which he hides at the bottom of the trash can every day, no matter how much I tell him honesty is the best policy, no matter how much I hammer him on his tennis technique, or being a good friend, or listening to a conversation instead of dominating it, or reminding him to stop following his impulses without regard for other people, or to sit up straight at the dinner table, or stop interrupting when other people are talking, and what's with the monologues or, rather, the endless rants . . . no matter what . . .

He loves me. He still kisses me and wants to touch my chubby cheeks, which are anything but chubby. He loves me unconditionally. What have I done for Duke? Nothing except be the poster girl for "Harried Mother."

SO WHAT IS BEAUTY?

I can answer that. It's in my eyes, the picture window I look through. It's eating Quinn's parmesan & rosemary popcorn after walking Emmie. Sometimes it's hiding in plain sight, like the note I found on my bed: "Mom, I am sorry I'm retarted, and can't be good for a week. From Duke." Sometimes it's a glass of Layer Cake cabernet with ice. It's the Statue of Liberty's right hand holding the torch, and the call from Jimmy, the man who's washed our car for the last fifteen years, telling me he bowled 300. It was Mom and Dad kissing in the shower three weeks before he died. This fall it was Morgan Freeman singing "That's Life" on the set of **Life Itself.** It was listening to Tom, the camera operator, tell me about the red barn he bought in upstate New York. It was the hairdresser Donna Marie's surprise wedding proposal from John, her partner of twelve years. It was Mikey, the makeup artist, whose wife took the big leap and jumped out of a plane at age fifty-eight. The thrill was so intoxicating, she forgot to open her parachute until it was almost too late. Crippled for the rest of her life, she said it was "worth it."

What is beauty? It was the recent healing-humor, funny-is-money phone call from Woody. "So, Half-Wit. The Golden Globes wanted to know where I could find someone stupid enough to come and pick up my Cecil B. DeMille Award, and all of a sudden it occurred to me, I don't know why, but your face in a beekeeper's hat came to mind." The next day he followed up with this: "I call you at ten to eight your time in the morning, and you're not in. I don't understand it. Where do you go at ten to eight in the morning? You're like a vampire. What is it with you? Look, after this appearance, maybe you'd start to get some roles as maids, or maybe maiden aunts, or a night watchman, or, who knows, one of those washer-women people, the kind that come in and clean the office after hours. Worm, call me back."

It's my brother Randy's long fingers as he toasts me on my sixty-eighth birthday with a cup of his favorite drink, instant coffee and Coke. It's my friend Larry, whose love I keep in my hip pocket. It's the other note I found on my bed: "Mom, Sorry! I want to be a better tennis player. So I left. Don't worry. I just want to play. I'm sorry you don't love me anymore. Love Duke." It's a knock on the door I don't answer. It's the two candy hearts I pick up off the floor that say, "Be mine." These are the sum of beauty's parts.

Diana Vreeland said she'd spent a lifetime looking for something she'd never seen. That's not a bad pursuit. Like Diana Vreeland, I regret what I haven't seen, but I'm thankful for what I have, and I promise myself this: I will try harder to look for what I don't see when it's staring me right in the eye.

SIZE TEN

Duke didn't say anything about the three hats on top of my head as he opened his presents Christmas morning. As we walked on Venice Boulevard, he didn't mention the henna tattoo I got with DUKE painted on my left hand and DEXTER on the right. At his birthday party in the Woodland Hills Sky High Sports trampoline center, he didn't mention my Rosie the Riveter ensemble with red bandanna, hoop earrings, and big, belted khakis rolled above my black Converse tennis shoes. He's ignored my recent habit of sporting swimwear apparel on the street: e.g., two long-sleeved Quiksilver crew-necked rash guards over Sea-a-Sucker board shorts with dark glasses and a hat. Every day I drive Duke to the bus stop with my Calvin Klein plaid men's pajama bottoms peeking out from under my black North Face Triple C full-length down coat. Every day my hair is in rollers. Duke has nothing to say about that, either.

These are my "save the best for the last," **Rebel Without a Cause** days. These are my "go for broke, grab anything you want to wear, because why not" days. Recently we went to dinner at Toscano to celebrate Dexter's passage from learner's permit to driver's license. I wore a pair of men's extra-large ski pants. Duke ignored them. He didn't care when I kicked off my six-inch Yves Saint Laurent platforms. When we toasted Dexter with Orangina in wineglasses, I bet Duke five dollars I could pick up my Visa card with my bare toes under the table. When I did, Duke went on an "It's so unfair, Cheeks" rant. "Cheeks, my cute little pie," he said, "my precious, my only squeaky in the whole wide world, you cheated. You did. You stuck your hands under the table and put the Visa card between your toes. That's cheating, Cheeks." I told him he was crazy. His response? Totally predictable: "This is a Mom Cheek fighting-to-cheat day. Admit it, Cheek Cheater. You cheated."

I knew I was breaking one of the cardinal rules the day I walked barefoot down the hallway of UCLA Lab School. But what the heck, I'd always wanted to feel the white speckled linoleum floor beneath my feet. I wondered if I could still grip a spoon off the floor with my toes and put it in my mouth, like I did when I was a ten-year-old wannabe contortionist. It would be tough, but I was convinced I could do it until I saw Judith Kantor, the librarian, heading in my direction. I immediately put on my concerned-parent face as I rushed over asking her about Duke's recent reading choices. What did she think of Rick Riordan, I asked, hoping she wouldn't glance down and see my Sally Hansen plaid toenails. Judith immediately launched into the pluses and minuses of Riordan's popularity. She paused for a second, then recommended Jack Ganto's **Dead End in Norvelt**. I kept up with a lot of "Oh, I see, yes, right. Right, of course! Right. That's such a great idea. Absolutely." Judith excused herself, saying she would email me a list of other recommendations. As if that wasn't enough, Norma Silva, the principal, suddenly waved hello. I waved back and made an immediate right turn into the janitor's closet, where I counted to sixty before going back out. I hurried to the Redwood Forest playground, where my toes rejoiced as they crunched through the redwood mulch. I sat on one of the kids' swings and pushed my arms back and forth as my feet flew through the air. It was perfect. That's when I spotted Duke playing dodgeball with his friends Zeke, Cassius, Evan, Atticus, and Ben. "Hey, Duke," I called, waving. Duke looked over, saw me, made a face, and ran away. When I went up to him he acted like he didn't know me. When we walked to the car he lagged three yards behind. In the car, he refused to sit shotgun. Finally I said, "What's up? What's wrong?"

"Mom, how could you?"

"Could I what?"

"Come to school barefoot?"

Okay, I thought, here we go. It's over. The day I prayed would never come had finally arrived. I'd embarrassed Duke in front of his friends. But the weird part, the part I couldn't understand, was, why my feet? Why not my overbearing personality, my Bozo the Clown clothing choices, or my decrepit age? But no, I'd had the audacity to run through UCLA Lab School's Redwood Forest barefoot.

Did this mean the days of "Cheeks, my cute little pie, my precious, you are my only squeaky in the whole wide world" were gone for good?

What would I do without "Your cheeks are so soft I want to touch them for a morning snack. I want to bite them and crunch them, too. Say yes, and I'll activate your cheek"? I hoped it didn't mean he'd stop serenading me with "Cheeks" to Justin Bieber's "Baby." Did I really have to face the fact that Cheeks's feet were suddenly cringe-worthy?

As a little girl I squished sea anemones with my toes in tide pools. I loved the hot black pavement against my bare feet as we walked to Earl's Hamburger stand. It was endlessly fun to dig through the sand as hundreds of crabs wiggled around my toes. When I climbed the cliffs of Divers Cove, I never fell. I almost convinced myself I had flying feet, like Mercury, the swift-footed Roman god. Every other aspect of my body, including my brain, was hesitant, but not my feet. Never my feet.

Duke used to like to go barefoot, too. But now that he's almost thirteen, his feet have begun to find themselves inside shoes more often than not. I guess the point is . . . Duke is growing up, and he doesn't want to draw attention to his feet or, most of all, his mother's feet. I understand. I have to face it. Duke is changing. Hey, when I reached those teen years I changed, too. The difference is, I began to frame my feet so they would become part of what I considered great design. That meant I fell in love with shoes.

Even then I knew there was a problem. The problem with shoes is they're worn on feet, and feet are not positioned close enough to the head. That means to be properly viewed, the body must be seen from head to toe. I remember wearing the most spectacular pair of creamy two-toned brown-and-beige Tony Lama cowboy boots in **Annie Hall** never to be seen on film. Even to have been partially visible would have required a medium close-up of Annie Hall sitting with her boots on a table near her face, or even better, a close-up of Annie Hall cleaning her Tony Lamas in her kitchen sink.

The beloved Tony Lamas are still in my closet next to a pair of Doc Martens, near six pairs of platform shoes circa 1980. These shoes, as well as my brown patent leather lace-up oxfords, my saddle shoes from **Interiors,** and the high-heeled Converse black-and-white high-tops given to me by my friend Johnny Gale, the hair colorist, are stacked on one side of the closet. I still wear the Florsheim Imperial men's shoes, size 8D, that went with my long Ralph Lauren camel-hair coat. Across from the men's shoes are the boots, which take up most of my closet. In the nineties I bought a gorgeous pair of riding boots I couldn't pull over my high arches. I'm still waiting for the day they collapse. I've kept my old Fryes, and even a pair of butch Caterpillar hiking boots. I love my chunky black patent leather boots with yellow and black polka dots from the disco era, too.

People can trash high heels all they want: they're impossible to walk in, they serve no purpose. This is completely unfair, and frankly not true. Never forget that Marilyn Monroe played baseball wearing heels. Ginger Rogers danced backward in them with Fred Astaire. And Pamela Anderson was booted off **Dancing with the Stars** wearing—that's right—a pair of high heels. Look, maybe "high-heeled beauty is pain," maybe it's expensive, but every woman needs one pair of genius high heels. I have a pair of seven-inch Christian Louboutin Red Medicines. That's what I call them, because that's what they are; they're red medicine. They're like a great glass of Layer Cake cabernet with ice. When I wear them I'm a contender. I'm a six-foot-two stilt walker, not some five-foot-seven excuse for a woman.

Once in a while a gal owes herself this kind of fix. In 1997 I saw a pair of orange herringbone Prada pumps in **Vogue**. I had to have them. As everyone knows, a pair of Prada anything is not cheap. So take my advice, slow down, way down, before you swipe your credit card. One more piece of advice: Don't be impulsive. Here's another: When in doubt, stick with black. Black will never disappoint. And always remember to accessorize. Don't be timid. Paint those toenails and sticker them up. Embrace your arches. Don't shy away from toe rings and ankle bracelets, either. Learn to take compliments. I haven't, but you should. Compliments linger. Someone once compared my legs to Lucille Ball's great gams. Like I cared. She was old. Now it's my turn to be old. If someone said the same thing to me today I'd be overjoyed. One more tip: Save your shoes. Save them all. Mark my words, you'll revisit wearing them sooner than you think. Plus, they're stimulants. Like music, they can take you back to certain moments, certain people, certain memories. I remember Dad's arches lifting into the air as he dove off the cliff at Dana Point. I remember seeing Pina Bausch's barefoot dancers pound a stage covered in dirt. Once I subscribed to CHARforce's Sexy High Arches website to see its Celebrities Assorted Slideshow honoring Meryl Streep's and Kate Hudson's and other actresses' outstanding high-arched feet. I wish I'd made the cut.

These days I'm not making the cut with Duke either. He'd never once said a word about my shoes, or my feet for that matter—not one thing—until that fateful day in the Redwood Forest. Was his humiliation provoked by Zeke or Atticus and the rest of his gang of six? It's hard to say. Was it because I broke a school rule, was that it? And, most important, at least for me: Was Duke ever going to forgive me? Was this mortification going to fester in his memory bank forever?

A week later I asked Duke if he wanted to go for a Sunday evening jog around Drake Stadium, on the UCLA campus. He was up for it. I wore my North Face parka. As always, it dragged across the track, and, as always, I carried a mug of Layer Cake cabernet with ice. I never jog without a chaser of red wine on the rocks. This time I didn't wear my Nikes. I deliberately went barefoot. Sure enough, Duke insisted I put my shoes on. When I asked why, he refused to elaborate. And there you have it. The onset of puberty. The end of childhood. I guess it's time to say goodbye to my bare feet, at least in front of Duke.

My podiatrist, Dr. Hakim, has also informed me that my barefoot days are over. If I choose otherwise, he assures me, I should be prepared for more broken toes and ankles, and bruises and sprains. He threatened me with stories of nails lying in wait and, worse—far worse—staph infections that could lead to my demise. Of course, he had no idea I'd been a wild child on the cliffs of Laguna Beach, a pioneer rolling down the sand-duned banks of Death Valley. He couldn't possibly know how much fun it was to howl in laughter at Woody, a.k.a. the White Thing, as I watched him step out of the shower onto a dozen clean white towels. The day he wore shoes as we held hands on an idyllic sandy beach in Puerto Rico did me in. Who wants feet that only know the feel of a satin sheet, or a soft slipper, or a sock? Poor Wood, he'll never know what he's missing. I'm proud my feet are not always shrouded in camouflage, or cloaked in protective gear, like every other square inch of my body.

In the end, I love shoes, but I love my feet more. My feet—the feet Bertram Ross, Martha Graham's heroic lead dancer, once told me were "fine examples of the perfect arch"; the feet that walked my sobbing body down a narrow hallway in **Reds** to my husband, John Reed, dying on a hospital bed; the feet that recently stood on our neighborhood bluff as the space shuttle **Endeavor** passed overhead on its final flight; the feet that tingled in fear as I stood holding hands with nine-year-old Duke as we looked over the edge of the observation deck at the Empire State Building.

Oh Duke, your only Chubby Roll of Cheek Dough Mom hopes you'll remember how much fun it was to jump into our swimming pool feet-first. I hope you won't forget running barefoot through the waves as you, Dex, and I stood on the beach witnessing Laguna's hurricane-force storm of 2007. Maybe. Maybe you'll remember our screams of laughter laced with fear as a nine-foot wave hit our feet on the deck of the old wooden lifeguard station in Fisherman's Cove. I wonder . . . I wonder if you'll remember me running barefoot in the mulch of the old Redwood Forest toward you, my only son. If so, maybe you'll forgive me for embarrassing you, with a shrug of the shoulders and a laugh. It was life, right, Duke? It was two bare feet transporting my body to you.

THE DREAM
OR THE
NEIGHBORHOOD?

THE IDEA

After renovating fifteen homes, I'm well acquainted with the subcontractors who don't show, the hardware that takes nine months to receive instead of the six weeks guaranteed, and the nightmare of opening up a wall only to find a dozen new stumbling blocks. After working for eighteen months on my last renovation, a Mission revival in Beverly Hills, my contractor, Ben Lunsky, was finished with my endless interruptions: "Wait a minute—what if we . . ." or "How about we try this?" or "Hey, Ben, I've got an idea." It all came to a head when I pulled him aside saying, "You know, we've got to cut costs, Ben. Things are getting out of hand. We need to—" Before I could finish, he blurted out, "Look, what can I do? Sorry, Diane, but you've got to face it. You're custom all the way, and you always will be!" I'd been around the block. I knew "custom" was short for "change-order queen." Ben wasn't wrong. On the eve of the recession we somehow managed to finish the house. Duke, Dexter, and I lived in it for a year, sold it at a loss, and rented Meg Ryan's Spanish-style home in Bel Air while I pondered a more reasonable approach to my housing obsession.

It was the end of an era. My serial renovation days were over. No more hunting down unattended gems, buying them, piling up expenses with an endless supply of "new ideas," and selling them at a profit. No more. That's what I kept telling myself, but like any other junkie, one day I had another "new idea," a big one. It came to me as I was pinning a cool image tagged as "staircases" by c ktnon, a graphic designer on Pinterest who has a couple million followers. At that moment, I decided the only way to get over being called "custom" was to embrace it. What could be more custom than building a new house? I justified the fantasy by telling myself I would be taking on a housing experience that demanded a practical approach. It would be a "how to" learning endeavor. And maybe in the end, if I did my homework and stuck with a budget—if I minded my p's and q's, whatever that means— I could build a sensible dream house from the ground up for the three of us. So I bought a half-acre lot on a street called Riviera Ranch Road in Sullivan Canyon.

Shortly thereafter, a young couple purchased Meg's house. They weren't interested in extend-ing the lease. Their lawyers notified us that we would need to leave at the end of the month. In a panic, Aileen Comora, my broker, and I looked at dozens of long-term rentals, and every house on the market. I was seriously freaking out. Plus I'd already invested the bulk of my savings in the unbuilt dream house, so I couldn't exactly go hog wild. Several homes had the stamp of previ-ous lives within their walls. As nice as they were, I couldn't live in the residue of someone else's life. When we saw a clean, bright two-story spec house in the Palisades offered at the right price, I passed. I dismissed it as cookie-cutter. There was no way Duke, Dex, and I would fit into a de-veloper's dream of the Connecticut Family Life-style. Another couple of weeks went by with no new possibilities. Aileen convinced me to take another look at the spec. It faced a public plaza in a neighborhood of nice but not exorbitantly priced houses. There were California bungalows, adorable haciendas, and a few Cliff May knock-offs built in the 1960s. They reminded me of my early California days, with Mom and Dad. What the heck . . . Duke, Dexter, our dog Emmie, and I had to live somewhere. Time was closing in. So I bought it. I did. I bought the brand-new opposite-of-custom Connecticut farmhouse one block from a sliding bluff that overlooks the Pacific Ocean.

THE NEIGHBORHOOD

We moved onto Wynola Street, across from Almar Plaza, eight months ago. In the center of the plaza stands a gnarly old spruce tree with king-sized roots that spread to the edge of the two-thousand-square-foot park. There are two bright blue plastic swings in the shape of an airplane hanging from the branches, just like the one in which baby Dexter used to scream in glee every time I pushed her higher. The play area is sprinkled with some sorry irises and a couple of bushes. A polished granite bench dedicated to the memory of Olive and John Thomas rests off to the side. The neighbor directly across from us is a retired Dodgers baseball player. His house has a widow's walk with a view of the ocean. Unlike him and his family, we do not have a widow's walk, but my bedroom faces east, and the sun enters my window when it rises, and the moon does, too. When I walk Emmie at six A.M., the moon, on its last legs, gently performs its disappearing act. Every morning I'm reminded of the mystery. Good morning, moon. Good morning, Dex. Good morning, Duke.

Our next-door neighbor Liz is the glue of the community. It was Liz who knocked on the door with a plate of cookies soon after we moved in, welcoming my family to the neighborhood. Her house, a wood-planked English cottage with an authentic (now illegal) shake roof, is irresistible. Every morning Emmie and I pass by. And every morning I elaborate on the same daydream. What if Liz were to put it on the market? What if I bought it? What if I connected her authentic cottage with my fake Connecticut farmhouse? Taking it a step further, what if Laurie, the landscaper next door on the other side, sold me her one-story 1950s modern? I could potentially amalgamate the three homes with interconnecting breezeways and a California cactus garden lined with oaks and olive trees. I assured myself I would be doing the neighborhood a service by linking three distinct examples of Los Angeles's "wacky" residential architecture into one. That's when a tiny voice in the furthest reaches of my brain asked: What about Liz and Laurie? What about the Glue and the Landscape Gardener?

Unlike Beverly Hills and Bel Air, our neighborhood does not have eight-foot walls blocking the intrusion of a community. Sometimes I sit on the swing, checking out the seasonal changes of the Santa Monica Mountains, and catch a glimpse of the ex-Dodger. His house, like mine, is spec all the way. When he shuts the door to his SUV and limps to his red front door, I worry about his injury. What happened? His windows are always closed. His curtains are often drawn. Talk about opposites. Our house, with its "We're Glad You're Here" greeting painted in white across the charcoal gray wall of the dining room, visible from the street, tells a different story. Our house has one demand, and it sums up my character. "Please look at me." Every now and then, the ex-Dodger will turn around and say "Hi, neighbor." I often wonder—and I'm sure I'm wrong—if what he really wants to say is "Hey, lady, what's with the 'All the world's a stage' living style?"

Last Christmas, Hi Neighbor was the brunt of a disgruntled observation from Mr.—excuse me—Dr. Harold Greene: "I apologize for your neighbor's horrible taste." Of course, I knew what the doctor was referring to. Who didn't? It was the Walmart blow-up Santa Claus on Hi Neighbor's porch. Every three minutes Santa bent over, and every three minutes his Santa pants fell to the ground, exposing his bare-ass Santa butt with "Merry Christmas" written across the cheeks. For a man of culture, this must have been the height of bad taste. But why tell me? Is it possible that the doctor missed the eight-foot-high address numbers I painted in black next to my front door? After all, he was talking to the woman with the look-at-me open-curtain policy. As the doctor sauntered off, I felt the urge to knock on Hi Neighbor's door and let him and his family know I had their backs. I wanted to reassure them that Santa's Christmas greeting will be welcomed back next year in all its bare-ass naked wonder.

One block down lives Lucille. It's hard not to adore Lucille. For one thing, she's a fellow baby boomer; for another, she has a disarmingly sunny outlook. Her home, a sweet, if modest gray ranch house with white trim, reflects Lucille's kindhearted character. She drives a '76 four-door green Mercedes. Every time I spot Lucille, she's either just about to open her car door or is cruising slowly past our house on her way to the drugstore, shouting, "I'm heading for CVS. Need anything, Diane, some odds and ends?" I think of Lucille as Almar Plaza's official greeter. The last time I saw her waving from the car, I was reminded of an old Carol Burnett appearance on **The Tonight Show** where she seemed to be promoting a kind of Pollyanna view on the merits of smiling. I remember her telling Johnny Carson, "The shortest distance between new friends is a smile." It's interesting how Lucille has made me reconsider Carol Burnett's proposition. If you think about it, a smile can be something more than a passing gesture given to, say, the gas station attendant putting air in your tires. Sure, it's a gesture, but a gesture can have a lasting effect. Lucille is my everyday optimist, my very own Carol Burnett. She reminds me to be grateful for the gift I was given, the big one: the gift of life.

THE DREAM

When I was a girl, my Sunday school teacher told us that if we believed in Jesus we'd live in a beautiful mansion in heaven. I believed her. At first I thought God would give me a castle made of stone, like in Walt Disney's **Snow White and the Seven Dwarfs**. A little later I changed my mind and wanted a replica of Hearst Castle. When I was twelve, Dad began taking me on tours through model homes in Orange County. Once we drove all the way to Costa Mesa, where we saw a high-end tract development called Vista del Rey Estates. "Estates" was a new word for me. I liked it. I wanted an estate, too. On the spot I told God I'd changed my mind about Hearst Castle—too fancy—and put in an order for Vista Del Rey's

$59,999 tract home, Plan A, in Costa Mesa. I was sure God didn't mind change orders—not that I knew yet what a change order was, but you get the drift. Anyway, I was convinced that he made zillions of homes that fit everyone's desires, including a special mansion for our recently demised cat Charcoal. I figured Charcoal probably chose the Plan B Cat House, which included a mountain of catnip and a limitless supply of fake mice.

905 NORTH WRIGHT STREET

Dad bought our very own tract house in 1958. It wasn't a model home, but it did feature four bedrooms and two baths. The wood-planked beige exterior included a two-car garage. As for curb appeal, there was none, unless you call one recently planted tree without leaves, a dirt-covered front yard, and two cars parked in the driveway curb appeal.

Over dinners of Mom's meat loaf with walnuts, Dad dominated the conversation with reports on success stories of real estate developers like Bill Krisel in the San Fernando Valley, who single-handedly mapped out the ABC's of proper planning for tract-style complexes. At the very mention of "proper planning," my mind wandered to what kind of ice milk—not to be confused with ice cream—we'd be getting for dessert; anything, anything but Neapolitan. The "in-teeer-resting" thing (that's how Dad pronounced it) about Bill Krisel's stair systems was that they were prefabricated in factories and installed on-site, thus allowing builders to offer lower prices.

The day that Walt Disney announced he was opening a new attraction in Tomorrowland called "Monsanto's House of the Future," Dad read us the details out of **The Orange County Register** over Mom's Sunday night taco dinner. Made entirely of plastic, right down to the electric toothbrushes, Monsanto's house had a kitchen with a state-of-the-art dishwasher, as well as a new type of heating device called "the Microwave." Mom laughed when she heard "The kitchen got dinner itself." The very next week, all six of us stood in line with hundreds of others waiting to take a tour of the "House of the Future." Since I was certain it would be my next change order for the perfect home in heaven, you can imagine my surprise when I saw what looked like an enormous wheel of cheese that seemed to pop out of the earth. Once we were inside "Plasticland," as Randy called it, I thought the vinyl kitchen countertops and the vinyl flooring and the vinyl bathroom splashes looked fake. I didn't care about the zillions of gadgets, or even the button that sprayed the scent of roses throughout the house. It was so sterile I had to be excused, and for the first time, I sort of understood that there was a difference between my idea of beauty and someone else's. For Dad, beauty was the ingenuity of Monsanto's engineers, but it could also be found in Mr. Bill Krisel's clever cost-cutting advances.

For a homemaker in the suburban 1950s, beauty was a purchasable commodity. That meant it was a product. Shopping for Mom was, unfortunately, limited by the family budget. She valiantly implemented her dreams by making our house on Wright Street an exhibition site. Her source for inspiration came from window displays, and her favorite displays were found at Bullocks Wilshire department store during the Christmas season. Inside the diorama glass boxes, mannequins in red scarves and wool coats gathered around the perfectly lit Christmas tree, where gift-wrapped presents, some open, some not, revealed Madame Alexander dolls, electric train sets, candy canes, and shiny new bicycles. I always looked for Mom's response before having mine. If her eyes lit up, if she was silent, I could see the dream begin its formation. Mom loved looking, and looking made her love the dream— the dream of beauty. But what was beauty? For Mom it was all things HOME.

Since she couldn't buy what she wanted, Mom

had to construct her own version. Sure, she stole ideas, but what else could she do? I don't know anyone who hasn't been guilty of trying to usurp beauty in one form or another. I like to think of stealing—or **appropriating**—as a way to create your own version of beauty, especially since it's based on an idea of someone else's idea of an idea. Get it? Everything I wanted from beauty was lifted from Mom and Dad. Everything. As I grew older, I began to believe that for both of them beauty was a feeling more than anything else.

HOME THEN

My childhood home, 905 North Wright Street, was the second house in from the cross street. Judy Reed lived on the corner. Judy and I played with our Barbies well over the designated stop age of twelve. Judy was an only child whose father was the principal of Santa Ana High School. One afternoon Judy and I got caught in the closet dressed up in her mother's clothes. Mr. Reed took my hand and marched me over to our house, where he told Mom point-blank that he thought it was strange that two girls age twelve were in a closet together. He didn't use the L-word, but he implied that there was something highly fishy going on. I was never again allowed in Judy's house.

Rocky Lee lived way down at the end of the street. He was Randy's best friend. One day I caught them under the bed looking at women's breasts in a **Playboy** magazine. I immediately told Mom. Mom spoke to Rocky's mom, which led to an intervention with all the other moms in the neighborhood. The subject? "Intercourse." One thing I learned: Never rat out your brother. It wasn't worth it.

Laurel and Bill Bastendorf lived next door. They had a pool with a sign outside saying, "We don't swim in your toilet. Don't pee in our pool." Their backyard was a jungle, like out of Maurice Sendak's **Where the Wild Things Are.** But that was nothing compared to the murder committed five blocks away, in one of the houses that had the same Plan B style as ours.

Lou lived across the street. She knew how to blow smoke rings. She was married to Jimmy G., who looked like a Ken doll. Lou couldn't have babies, so she let me stay overnight in her former Plan A model home every other Friday. Jimmy G. made brown drinks with ice in tumbler glasses. After three brown drinks, Lou and Jimmy G. turned out to be a lot of fun. I was given 7Up in a tall green glass with a dozen red cherries on top and lots of ice. I decided that once I got to heaven I would request the very same tall glasses, with the same red cherries, and a barbecue on the patio, and a cook's hat, and a fancy apron, and lots of laughter shared with people like Lou and Jimmy G.

Before moving to the Palisades, I'd forgotten 905 North Wright Street, and how happy our family was to share the common bond of being part of a neighborhood. I'd forgotten that those were the best of times for all of us, Mom included. Randy and I produced our first Hall Family Talent Show, where we all played monsters who sang and danced to "Monster Mash." Every spring Mom gathered a group of neighbors to go see the swallows return to Capistrano. Dad shared Saturday night beers with Bill from next door. The skinny trees in our front yards matured. We were part of a community that shaped the kind of people we became. When several blocks of houses south of Wright Street were leveled so that Interstate 5 could pass through, it left a gaping hole in our neighborhood. Sure, we continued to eat dinners at the counter while Dad, as always, monopolized the conversation, but one night he told us he was going to quit his job. He said he was revving up his engines in order to start an independent engineering firm to be called Hall and Foreman, Inc. That's when I knew a change was going to come.

CHANGE

The next year, I was accepted at the Neighborhood Playhouse School of the Theatre, in New York City. Suddenly I lived on the fifth floor of a brick walk-up with a toilet down the hall. From there, I went from one studio apartment to another for seven years. There was no neighborhood to be found in New York City, at least not for me. Every morning I opened the door, closed the door, and locked the door behind me. Every day I joined millions of other New Yorkers on the street. Every night I unlocked my door, closed it behind me, and that was it.

After the success of **Annie Hall,** I bought a tower apartment on the twenty-first floor of the San Remo, on Central Park West. It was hard to believe I lived in a wraparound sky house with a 360-degree view of the city. I was in my early thirties. I'd achieved my goal. I lived in a dream house. But it wasn't enough. I began to look at **Architectural Digest, House and Garden,** and **The World of Interiors.** My tear-sheet days had begun in earnest. I began collecting books with names like **The 70s House**, and **Frank Lloyd Wright: His Life, His Work, His Words.** Years later, after Dad got sick, I moved to Los Angeles and launched into a life of buying, selling, and living in a series of houses.

L.A., like New York, was not neighborhood-friendly. Sure, people lived in houses next door, down the block, and around the corner, but no one, not one person, rang my doorbell the way, years later, Liz did, with a plate of cookies. But who was I to talk? I never rang a doorbell welcoming a new family to the neighborhood.

It didn't matter. I was dream-house bound, dream-house inspired, and dream-house obsessed. Today I actually sat down and counted how many apartments and houses I've rented, bought, and sold. Close to fifty. Even after I adopted Dex and then, five years later, Duke, it was always the next house, the next remodel, the next Spanish, the next Lloyd Wright, the next project with the next promise of what? My very own exceptionally perfect display-case model home? It never entered my mind that I might be reliving those early days with Dad's hand in mine as we walked through model homes. It never did. I never thought about Mom and those inspirational visits to Bullocks Wilshire in downtown Los Angeles.

Last week I was at Big Daddy's Antiques off Jefferson in Culver City, looking at a fourteen-foot dining room table to fit in the fifteenth house Dexter's lived in during the eighteen years of her life, and the tenth house Duke's lived in during the thirteen years of his. What am I doing? And why?

One-fourth of those eighteen years were spent in a variety of pit-stop rentals while I pursued the next Lloyd Wright (there were two), the next Wallace Neff, the next Paul Williams Spanish, or the surprise Mission Revival by Ralph Flewelling—even the Windsor Smith house in Mandeville Canyon, which fell out of escrow. Behind and in front of my back, people have called me a serial renovator, a serial flipper, even a wannabe Ellen DeGeneres.

The moves, all fifteen, centered on the dream of a beautiful life lived in a beautiful home. As with all addicts, I found that each house fell short. Sure, they were the homes of my choice— the homes of little Duke and Dexter, who would become big Duke and bigger Dexter. And even though I renewed my vows with every residence, I couldn't beat the odds. The junkie in me prevailed. We moved.

I like to blame Dad for my inability to commit to HOME. I like to say, "Not my fault—it's in the DNA." I like to blame the feel of Dad's left hand in mine as we walked through those early model homes described by D. J. Waldie in his essay on Maynard Parker, the photographer for **House Beautiful,** as "The Station Wagon Way of Life," where "Pace Setter houses made sub-urban dreams a reality." Subconsciously, I knew that suburban dreams of Pace Setter houses had to be in multiples. One would never be enough.

In a way, each and every house had the ulti-mate say. True, I bought and remodeled them. I raised the ceiling heights at Copa de Oro Road. I resurfaced the fireplaces at 820 North Roxbury. I changed the Italianate exterior to its more orig-inal Mission Revival façade, and turned the en-trance into a library. But no matter what I did to each house, its essence remained intact.

With this in mind, I forgive myself for con-tinuing the pursuit of the unattainable. I know I'm guilty of dragging my kids all over the West Side of Los Angeles as we moved from rental to new house, ad infinitum. I hope they develop their own love of the built world. Like army brats, they seem to have adjusted to life on the go every two years or so. That's what I tell myself, anyway. But sure, I question my motives. Working on a renovation is honoring the past by including it in the future. For me, it's the process, not the result. The result is always the same. When do I start the next one? What harm is there in clean-ing them up, reusing them, only to send them on their way? I've given people jobs. I've sold the product. The houses still stand.

Every day, each and every one of us experiences a series of losses. I walk Emmie to the bluff, where I see a stranger walking his dog. We pause and smile. Our dogs chase tennis balls. I never see him or his dog again. In my car on Sunset, I notice a woman putting on lipstick as she texts on the phone while driving. She's gone before I can honk my horn. I have a meal at Giorgio Baldi. I order that exact meal two weeks later, but it's not the same. Nothing is ever the same. Nothing is permanent. Nothing can be trusted to be there. Nothing is safe, including home. Why lie to yourself? Every day we leave something, someone, some observation behind.

I've faced the truth. No dream can live up to its expectations. Ownership is brief; in fact, it's a fiction. And beauty? Beauty is a discovery that diminishes the truth of reality. So keep looking.

THE DREAM OR THE NEIGHBORHOOD?
The point is . . . I'm not sure what I'm going to do. Should we move out of the neighborhood after the dream house is built? In a year Dexter will have graduated from high school, and Duke—oh my God, Duke will be in his final year of middle school. Emmie will be fourteen years old. Where does it all go? Come on, Diane, you've got to give up something. What's it going to be, the Dream or the Neighborhood?

A few weeks ago, Heidi, who lives on Muskingum Place, knocked on my door to tell me that fifty-seven-year-old Michael, with the two black dogs and the twelve-year-old adopted boy, had died. He collapsed in his home. That's it? You wake up one morning. Everything is normal. Everything is taken for granted. Your wife and son are in the kitchen eating breakfast, while you're dying in the bedroom? The terms are incomprehensible. Enjoy the tragedy of your life, Joseph Campbell said. Do I have to? What if I die before the dream house is built? Will I regret the unbuilt dream I left behind? Or is death the end of regret? When my friend John Burnham was robbed at gunpoint in the carport of his home, one thought came to my mind: Why hadn't he spent all his money? Life is a risky business, a now-or-never situation. The Dream or the Neighborhood?

Eventually I will have a choice. Do we live in a house on a block with proper streetlights, plenty of No Parking signs, and an alarm system banner posted outside my walled-in compound? I won't have to worry about "Breaking News" of unfolding neighborhood dramas. No Liz. No Lucille, No Hi Neighbor, either. I'll be able to get up and go to sleep in the presence of unobstructed beauty, or at least my idea of it. Undoubtedly a couple of years will pass, I'll sell the dream home while in the process of building another, then another, and another, if I'm lucky. What's wrong with that?

Several friends have advised me not to build at this age. They say I don't need the pressure. They say, "Enjoy your life." They say, "Calm down, Diane, you're on the brink of becoming another Sarah Winchester." Sleepless nights worrying over imagined change orders and repeating the word "custom" as if it were a mantra is a waking nightmare. But I'm determined to live in the result even if it turns out to be one more ridiculous "folly" lining the streets of Los Angeles. Hey, I took the tour of the infamous "Winchester Mystery House," so I know about the crazy heiress Sarah Winchester. I heard the stories of the psychic who advised her to beware of the spirits of the people who had been killed by Winchester rifles. Sarah's only recourse was to move west and build a house to be shared with a group of restless ghosts. Convinced that they would kill her if she completed construction, Sarah Winchester spent her entire fortune on round-the-clock construction, 24 hours a day, 7 days a week, 365 days a year, for the next 38 years. I'll never forget walking through rooms with doors that opened into walls, staircases that led nowhere, and windows that looked onto concrete blocks. Let me just say I was impressed, not only by the will of the woman but also by her 160-room house. I mean, come on. That's taking an idea very far.

I'm intrigued by every screwball who built a structure that took "dream house" to the limits of possibility. Los Angeles alone has succeeded in being home to a multitude of so-called follies, built in an atmosphere free from the constraints of education and good taste. I have no doubt my house will fit into our city's melting pot of confections. I'm not ashamed to admit I get a kick out of the thirty-thousand-square-foot Mc-Mansions I drive by in the flats of Beverly Hills. I love the Dutch Colonial Revival covered with every concrete animal God placed on Noah's Ark in pairs. I'm inspired by building a fantasy of a fantasy fostered on a dream of a past that never was. This includes great architects as well. Think of John Lautner's Chemosphere house. It looks like a spaceship posed on a hilltop in Hollywood. Think of Tony Duquette's abandoned synagogue, which he restored and renamed "the Duquette Pavilion of Saint Francis." Don't forget the Petal House, by Eric Moss, who remodeled a tract home by adding a second story using composite shingle siding, then fooled around with the roof and peeled back four triangles, setting them at different angles so they looked like petals on a flower. Or the Struckus House, by Bruce

Goff, which, swear to God, appears to be a giant-sized eighteenth-century birdcage.

I know that Los Angeles is ridiculed for creating the most deviant concoctions of what people call home. Great. I mean it. Great. I'm buying it, hook, line, and sinker, and I don't care if my misguided obsession is frowned upon. I don't. At least I have a dream of beauty, no matter how inappropriate. Here in Los Angeles, I have the right to pursue happiness. Homes included. My idea may not be yours—or anyone's, for that matter—but it's mine. After all, I'm Jack Hall's daughter. I love figuring things out—granted, my way. I'm Dorothy Hall's daughter, too, and I love all things HOME.

For now, Dexter, Duke, Emmie, and I live in a neighborhood. Our house with its floor-to-ceiling glass doors and jumbo-sized black numbers painted outside is an open book. Every night our neighbors can see our good times and bad times, if they choose. Every morning they can ride their bikes past our nothing-to-hide kitchen. After the rain last night, Emmie and I got up for our walk to the bluff, where we saw the Pacific, the largest of the earth's oceanic divisions, extending from the Arctic in the north to the Antarctic Ocean in the south. The Pacific covers one-third of the earth's surface. To me, and I'm sure Emmie, too, it is the first wonder of the world. It is not man-made. It is not a dream house; nor was it built in the likeness of God. What is it? Inexplicable beauty. After the same walk in the morning, as we turn our backs to take up the tasks of the day, I call Stephanie and leave a message: "Did you hear about the landslide last night? The houses on the rim are fine, and thank God the Aloha Courtyard Trailer Park residents are okay, too. That rim is scary. Emmie, the idiot, almost fell over the edge. But, wait a minute, I forgot—do I pick up Duke at extended day or what? Call me back."

"What kind of house would you like to live in?" I asked Duke when he was little. "A house with people in it," he said. "A house with people in it? Not a dream house?" "Nope. A house with people in it, Mom."

I don't know if it's a good idea to pull up roots again. Maybe Wynola should be our permanent home. But then, what's permanent? Not 905 North Wright Street, now long gone. Heart-breakingly, not Mom and Dad, either. What ever happened to Lou and her husband, Jimmy G.? What about Judy Reed? She has to be in her mid-sixties, and Bill and Laurel, where are they? Even now Duke wants to live in a house with people in it. Dexter likes the neighborhood. So do I. People make up a neighborhood. People. But people are not dream homes. People are not set in stone. They're not brick and mortar, or board and batten. People do not have the capacity to withstand time.

Emmie and I are looking at Laurie's new lawn when Janice, who owns a prefab in the Aloha Courtyard Trailer Park, passes me, saying she's not worried. "The bluff will stand firm," she tells me. At least for now. I nod and think: Risk taker—that's what she is, a risk taker living at the edge. Aren't we all? When I get home, I put the dog leash away, rinse out my coffee cup, and see Lucille at the door. She's got the Pilates brochure she was talking about a few days ago. I smile my best greeter smile, not as big as hers, and think: Irreplaceable. The woman is irreplaceable. As my smile widens, I know it's a beautiful life in the moment, especially on Wynola Street. There's no chance we are leaving, at least not for now.

OLD
IS GOLD

Last summer I was making a movie in Bridge-port, Connecticut, with Rob Reiner and Michael Douglas. I had the day off and decided to take the train into New York City to see my friend Kathryn.

When I got out of the shower I made the mistake of glancing in the mirror. My body, the whole "kit and caboodle," as my Grammy Hall would have said, is falling. I've been aware that it was collapsing since Fiona Lewis, a fellow actress and the wife of producer Art Linson, scared the shit out of me back in the late 1980s when she confronted me at the Chateau Marmont about the way my butt had dropped. She pointed to hers, saying she was heartbroken. Not being a booty aficionado, I had no idea mine had taken a plunge, nor did I care. I was, however, concerned about my face, and decided to take my friend Candy Bergen's advice. I went to see Janet Sartin, a renowned cosmetologist. When I opened the door to her private consultation room, I found a gurney in the middle of what looked like the set of **Frankenstein,** the old one, the one starring Boris Karloff, complete with microscopes, smoking jars, and chemical compounds.

It was all very unexpected, but not as unexpected as Janet Sartin, who put me on the gurney, got down to business, and gave me the bad news. I looked a little "worse for the wear"—that's how she put it. The multitude of scars on my cheeks from basal cell carcinoma treatments didn't help. I had dangerously dry skin, she said, and my eyes were drooping. With that, she began massaging me with jolts from some sort of wand. I didn't remember having made an appointment for shock therapy. As if that wasn't enough, when I left I looked just as tired as when I'd arrived.

The friendly ticket agent at the Stamford train station recognized me and smiled. I smiled, too, saying I wanted a ticket to Grand Central Terminal, and gave him a twenty. He handed me back twelve dollars, along with a senior/Medicare discount stub. Only a few days before I'd bought a ticket for Brad Pitt's **World War Z** and had been given a senior discount as well. That's two in one week. I suppose it wasn't the worst thing in the world, but it sure did feel like it.

Standing on the platform, waiting for the express, made me nervous. What if I got on the wrong train? I was afraid to ask the woman next to me. She must have been in her late fifties. Her mouth turned down at the ends. Not exactly inviting, and her hair was bottle black. I wondered when she'd gone "hard." When was the moment her face became set in stone like Grammy Hall's?

I couldn't remember a time when Grammy wasn't old. She defied people's perception of "over the hill," partially because she didn't give a hoot what anybody thought. She kept her mind on the p's and q's, which to her meant money. That's the way Grammy's life rolled, in cash: in fives and tens and twenties and fifties; in one-hundred-dollar bills stuffed under her bed in rolled-up blankets, suitcases, and lockboxes. Her kitchen shelves were decorated with jam jars filled with pennies, nickels, dimes, quarters, and silver dollars she won playing the slots every weekend in downtown Vegas. She claimed banking was for " 'tards"—retards. Grammy Hall was not warm and fuzzy. In short, she was a walnut you couldn't crack. I can't recall a time when she hugged me, or wiped away my tears. She was independent to a fault. I admired her for sticking to her guns, man or no man. When Dad became successful as a civil engineer, she didn't pat him on the back and say, "I'm so proud of you, son." Oh no. There was none of that. She relentlessly compared her ability to earn money with his, pointing out that she was an unmarried woman with no education who had single-handedly made her way in the world. She insisted that he consider the setback of being born female in the late nineteenth century. According to her, these factors proved that she earned more than him by a walloping 15 percent. Yep, she was a ball breaker. On the other hand, Mary Hall was the reason Dad did so well in business. She knew the truth early on. Money is power. Money buys you independence. To her, what beauty there was to be extracted from this "weird old world" was green and wrinkled.

Once on the train, I took out my iPad and hit Pinterest, where I found an absolutely gorgeous portrait of Meryl Streep taken by Brigitte Lacombe. Why couldn't I have Meryl's patrician nose or Yale education? I was about to pin her when a couple of young women came up to me and asked to take a picture, saying how "cute" I was and how "totally adorable" I looked. I'd take anything, even "old lady," even "doddering," over "cute and adorable." The last thing I want to be is innocuous or cuddly, as in "harmless"!

I used to get stopped with "Are you Sandy Dennis?" or "You're what's her name, Jill Clayburgh? Right?" Last summer, a maid at the Four Seasons in Maui looked at me and said in recognition, "Firecracker?"

I shook my head. "Huh?"

She pointed at me. "Firecracker?"

I shook my head again and said, " 'Firework'?"

"You. Fireworks?!"

"No, I'm not Katy Perry."

Was she blind? I'm forty years older than Katy Perry. At the airport the next day, a teenage boy asked me if I was Jane Fonda. "No. No. Don't worry about it. I'm not Jane Fonda." Clearly I'm somebody, just not me.

As the train pulled into Grand Central, I grabbed my bag and hurried out. I had lived in New York City for twenty years, and yet Grand Central Terminal has never failed to stun me. Were it not for Jackie Kennedy, there would be no hundred-year-anniversary banners hanging on the walls because there would be no Grand Central Terminal. As I stood taking it all in, hundreds of people were rushing to catch trains, grabbing magazines, waving hello and goodbye. A middle-aged woman arm in arm with a beautiful old man in yellow shorts, a yellow shirt, and a Panama hat came up to me for a picture. I always say yes to people who ask for a picture if, and only if, they're willing to be in it with me. What's the point of having a picture of me without them? It has no meaning. It's abstract, and besides, it makes me feel good to be friendly. Like Sally Field, I'm grateful that they seem to like me. Maybe they don't, but I can't tell. It's a moment in time. A lovely experience. The woman was sweet, but Frank Zimmerman—that was his name— was perfection. At ninety-six he'd flown up from Boca Raton, Florida, to celebrate the birth of his seventh great-grandchild. Like Grand Central Terminal, he was a centenarian. Old, as in almost one hundred years old. Old-is-gold old.

Dave Gold was old, octogenarian old, when I met him at his granddaughter Genna's bat mitzvah. He reminded me of Walter Matthau, and Art Carney, too: the unassuming way he dressed; the way he loped along, kind of hangdog. His life was anything but hangdog. Dave dropped out of college at nineteen to run the family liquor store. He noticed that when he put a bottle of wine on sale for a dollar or ninety-eight cents, it sat on the shelves, but when he placed a ninety-nine-cent sign on the bottle, it was scooped up in no time. Ninety-nine became Dave's magic number. So much so, he had an epiphany. What if he created a store where everything cost ninety-nine cents? Despite his family's unanimous chorus of "that's a ludicrous idea," Dave stashed enough money away to launch his 99 Cents Only Stores at an age when most people are looking forward to the benefits of retirement. He was in his fifties.

Gold was the kind of guy who started work at 4 A.M. and finished at 7 P.M., his daughter Karen Schiffer said in his **Los Angeles Times** obituary. "He would come home at the end of the day and say, 'Look at this beautiful shampoo.' He would say, 'We have fifty truckloads of Kleenex coming in.'" And his ads were as outlandish as his personality. One congratulated the Dodgers on losing ninety-nine games. Another wished Joan Rivers a "Happy 99th Facelift."

Dave did not adopt the outward flash of a man whose 99 Cents Only dream expanded to more than three hundred stores, making him one of **Forbes**'s famous 400 richest. Hell no. He lived in the same middle-class home for five decades with Sherry, his wife of fifty-five years. I admired Dave Gold. He was an authentic eccentric who believed in his dream and stayed an original family man to boot. Last April, eighty-year-old Dave died at home, still doing business as usual. Old Grand Central. Old Frank Zimmerman. Old as gold Dave Gold.

There was nothing gold about the crumpled envelope I found in the pocket of my Marni dress this morning. It was almost as if it was waiting for me to toss it into the trash; instead I made the mistake of looking at the return address. Tim Nicholson, the Neptune Society, 4312 Woodman Avenue, Sherman Oaks, CA 91423. And guess what? Against my better judgment . . . I opened it.

"Dear Diane," the letter inside began. "For a variety of reasons, more and more people are choosing to plan for a memorialized cremation over a traditional funeral arrangement, and the numbers are increasing every year! Cremation just makes sense. If you are not interested in spending your family's inheritance on embalming, caskets, vaults, markers, fancy funeral homes or cemetery property, then we have the answer! To learn more about the Neptune Society and our different memorialization options, simply complete and return the enclosed reply card or visit www.neptunesociety.com."

And on and on and on. Cut to "Sincerely, Tim Nicholson." And: "P.S. Sometimes deaths happen before you have had a chance to put plans in place. Neptune stands ready to assist at a moment's notice should you need immediate help." As if that wasn't enough, Tim added, "Please accept our apologies if this letter has reached you at a time of serious illness or death in your family."

Serious illness? Death in the family? I know the time has come for me to contemplate preparation for the end of the road, the "see you later, alligator, till we meet again" part of my life. But do I have to so soon? How about in a while, or later, a lot later, and definitely not with Mr. Tim Nicholson's cost-cutting planned memorial cremation in mind.

That day in New York, I got into a cab and called Kathryn, who wanted to meet on the West Side at 110th Street so we could stroll through Central Park. As we walked arm in arm past the newly refurbished Charles A. Dana Discovery Center, people greeted us with "Beautiful day!" and "Great weather, huh?" The Conservancy Garden's roses were in bloom. On Fifth Avenue we saw the Museum of the City of New York's red-brick Georgian building and decided to go inside, where we found ourselves in front of **A Beautiful Way to Go,** an exhibition celebrating the 175th anniversary of Green-Wood Cemetery. We looked at Hudson River School paintings and historic documents from the old cemetery. When I stopped in front of a photograph illustrating a nineteenth-century headstone that read, "Grace Ann Small. Wife of William B. Small."

Suddenly five-foot, two-inch Grace Johansen came rushing to mind. Grace was the oldest person I've ever known. She must have been in her mid-eighties when I first saw her parading down Hollywood Boulevard, greeting tourists in front of Musso and Frank's restaurant. I was trying to find people to interview for a movie I was making on the subject of heaven. Over time, Grace and I became friends. We stayed friends until the day she died, at age ninety-seven. I would lay ten-to-one odds her funeral was a hell of a lot more fun than Grace Ann Small's.

First of all, the crowd bore no resemblance to the formal gatherings pictured at Green-Wood Cemetery. There was Carol Kane, Bud Cort, Joan the pet psychologist, Dr. David Kipper, Rhea Perlman, and Mae, Grace's Indonesian waitress at the Holiday Inn's coffee shop, where Grace dined every evening. Also in attendance was Mae's co-worker Raphael, the Mexican waiter who served her apple pie with coffee every morning, Roddy McDowell's sister, and Cameron Crowe, the director. People say Hollywood has no family, yet we were a family of friends gathered in honor of our beloved Gracie, who played a mean piano and packed a wallop with her song stylizations.

In the chapel at the Hollywood Forever Cemetery, the light shone on Grace's casket as we sang "Ain't She Sweet." Raphael stood up and spoke extemporaneously on the details of Grace's morning hot apple pie with coffee and cream. Mae talked about Grace's irrational fear of earthquakes and her love of Jean Naté perfume. Carol told a couple of Grace's favorite jokes. "What's a Honeymoon Salad?" "I don't know." "Lettuce be together. We're a peach of a pear. My heart beets for you."

A six-minute video montage was projected onto an old-fashioned pull-up screen where a pulpit would have stood. There were snapshots, beginning with young Grace all decked out at the piano, then one on the day she married Al, her husband of fifty years, and another of her playing the slots in Las Vegas, her favorite city. Then came the photographs of Grace with her extended family . . . us, celebrating a series of birthdays at the top of the Holiday Inn's famous revolving restaurant. Toward the end, there were photographs of ninety-six-year-old Grace wearing her new black acrylic wig. The same wig she wore as she lay dying in her hospital bed at the Motion Picture Home. I remembered holding her hand. It seemed as if she was working hard to live through dying. No more Jean Naté for little Gracie. No more Jean Naté. No more Grace.

Outside the chapel, we walked behind a vintage black hearse to the mausoleum, where Grace's simple green casket was draped with red roses. The grass was brown, the wilting palm trees slumped, and the little road winding its way through Hollywood Forever needed repaving. The mausoleum's skylights were missing sections of stained glass, and yet . . . there was something compelling in the disarray. It felt like we were in a post–World War II Fellini film, gallivanting through the ruins. What is it about abandoned buildings and overgrown cemeteries? What is it about the beauty of collapse? Is it something more than meets the eye? Maybe. Is it beauty caressed by loss?

As the sun faded and Grace was laid to rest, I couldn't help but see her face as she spoke to me before she died. This is what she said. She said she saw a miracle in the sky, a genuine miracle. Then she got serious and shook her head back and forth, saying, "I saw a cross in the sky. It was a real cross. But nobody looks up at the sky anymore, nobody looks up at the sky."

In honor of Grace, I make it my business to look up at the sky on occasion. To date I haven't seen a cross. But I do think life is a miracle. At this point I'm sure of one thing, and that's this: I know nothing. I would venture to say some of my friends would agree. At least I'm pretty sure they would concur that life is far more impenetrable than we imagined. This isn't Disneyland. It's Wonderland. Most of us over sixty have come to the point where we recognize that our accomplishments are diddly-squat in the grand scheme of things. I guess I have to admit that I'm in preparation for the incomprehensible end zone of life. I don't know if I have enough courage to stare into the spectacle of the great unknown. I don't know if I will make bold mistakes, go out in a blaze of glory unbroken by my losses, defy complacency, and refuse to face the unknown like the coward I know myself to be, but I hope so. On the way I intend to deepen my laugh lines and enjoy the underrated beauty of humor. Like Grace, I don't want to be "afraid to crack a joke. After all, it's only a can of people."

Thinking of Grace, I told Kathryn I wanted to go to Café Sabarsky for a double espresso in a glass with whipped cream and some apple pie. Fifth Avenue was swarming with people. I love Los Angeles. I live there, but I miss the energy of a city that houses 8.3 million people on an island two miles wide and thirteen and a half miles long. In front of the Guggenheim, I heard someone calling my name through the crowd. I looked over to see a stunning woman getting out of a limousine. "Diane, it's Ricky." "Oh my God, Ricky, you look great." And she did. Ricky Lauren, Ralph's wife, looked great. "No, Diane, no, you look great." But I didn't. I looked like a woman my age.

Cher once said, "There is only value to having the look you have when you are young and no value to the look you have when you are older." Who can argue with Cher? She's not wrong. But she's not right, either. What she is, is right for herself. Diana Vreeland claimed she approved of plastic surgery, noting that none of her friends could understand why she hadn't had it done herself. But, Vreeland added, she had her own reasons.

What were her reasons? I know what they were. They were hers. All of us over sixty-five have our reasons. I respect Cher's choices as much as I respect mine.

I tell myself I'm free to do whatever the hell I want with my body. Why not? I may be a caricature of my former self; I'm still wearing wide-belted plaid coats, horn-rimmed glasses, and turtlenecks in the summertime. So what? Nobody cares but me. I don't see anything wrong with face-lifts or Botox or fillers. They just erase the hidden battle scars. I intend to wear mine, sort of. At least that's what I say to myself.

Let's take the example of being in your sixties but looking forty, like Ricky. Kathryn wanted to know who Ricky was. "Duh! Ralph Lauren's wife." "Is it his second marriage?" I set her straight: "They've been married almost fifty years." We marveled at her great hair, thick and long; her dazzling smile; her straight-as-an-arrow patrician nose, so unfair; but most of all, her fantastic figure in her Ralph Lauren pantsuit. Okay. Okay. We agreed. What woman in her sixties doesn't want to look like Ricky Lauren? I do. But the awful truth is this: no matter what I do, I'm never going to look like Ricky Lauren. Kathryn and I are going to have to let that dream go. And we did. We made it to Sabarsky's. They didn't serve apple pie, but the strudel was delicious. Grace would have ordered it hot, with vanilla ice cream on the side. And Ricky Lauren? Ricky's beauty will always be high on my want list.

Yep. I belong to a group of sixty-five and older show business folk. Sometimes I wish I could talk to my contemporaries about how they're grappling with their senior years. Do they wake up every morning and, like me, look in the mirror with a big sigh? Do they? Do they ask themselves what old age is for? I do. I think I know the answer. It's for grace—not Grace my friend, but now that I think of it, Grace was a perfect example of generosity, goodwill, and poise, and isn't that what grace is? No one wants to be called doddering, or past their prime, or long in the tooth. No one wants to be reminded that they're no spring chicken. No one wants to be a dilapidated, broken-down, beat-up, out-of-date, cast-off, worn-out, stale example of a human being.

We worked hard to become who we are. But with the accolades behind, and the honors of the past in front, what is our present? For those of us who've been separated from reality by fame, being old is a great leveling experience. I don't mind being taken down a peg or two, but what about the physical effects?

Every one of us is going through bodily decline. We're less active. We have wrinkles and liver spots. Most of us, I would venture to say, have tried to remedy these unsightly problems. And why not? Our hair color has changed from black, brown, red, and yellow to gray and white all over. In most cases that, too, has been rectified—with the exception of Michael Douglas, who is one silver-haired fox. I am a sorry example of the truth that women, as well as men, are losing their hair. Not only do we have reduced circulatory system function but we're losing lung capacity, too. It's all pretty tragic. Our immune systems are shutting down, and I don't know about anyone else, but there are changes in my vocal cords that seem to be producing a strange "old person" voice, which I hate worse than my envy of Michael Douglas's hair. Every one of us has a heightened risk of injury from falls, hearing loss, diminished eyesight, and, yes, as if I didn't know it, we all have reduced mental abilities, too. Thanks for nothing.

I have become friends with some of my show business contemporaries. The most unlikely is Jack Nicholson. When I first met him, in my thirties, friendship was not possible. He was Jack Nicholson. I didn't want to be his friend. I wanted him to kiss me. It didn't happen. In my mid-fifties we met again, when Nancy Meyers cast us in **Something's Gotta Give.** On the set I listened to his stories about being raised in a beauty salon surrounded by women. He listened to mine. We commiserated about old friends and how to make new ones. We played around with the idea of forming a pseudo-salon in Los Angeles, where we would gather like-minded people to discuss topics of the day. Jack and I still meet every month or so for lunch at his home on top of a hill. His unassuming California ranch house, built in the 1960s, is filled with paintings by Henri Matisse, Picasso, Maynard Dixon, Andy Warhol, and Tamara de Lempicka.

A few years ago, I wrote him a little note of friendship. The sentiments remain the same today.

"I've been thinking about you and friendship," it began. "Here's what it means to me. It means from down here at the bottom of the hill to way up there at the top of the mountain, I'll be watching your back. I'll be looking out for you. Think of me as your Palisades rep, your gal Friday on the West Side.

"Unlike me, you are not a person who resides in the world of right and wrong. You are not bound by moral platitudes. Your authenticity has been earned by the choices you've made. These choices show on your face. Your face, your great face, challenges standardization. Looking at you for as long as I have has made it easy for me to come to the conclusion that your face is the best face I've ever seen. Not only because you're pretty—and you are pretty, Jack—but mainly because over the years your face has morphed into something magnificent. I believe that at the heart of this magnificence one would **not** find the bad boy genius actor who has dazzled us, but the good man. You may not like hearing this, but you are **a good man**. In spite of all your fame, talent, wealth, and temptation . . . you are a good man. You are **my** good man. And even though words like 'good' and 'decent' have come to represent sappy Hallmark cards . . . they mean everything to me, especially now that I'm older. Based on accumulated evidence collected over years of watching both of us rise, stumble, fall, and get up again, you remain a friend. As we plow headfirst into the so-called golden years I continue to think, rethink, and re-rethink you. It's been a great challenge. My interest in you will never decline. As the years go by, like I said before, I'll be watching your back and, might I add, loving you from down here."

Kathryn had to get back home. I had a few hours to kill, so I took a chance and called Woody. He was about to leave for France to make a movie, something he's done virtually every year since 1965. What could we do together before he headed off? I asked him if he wanted to take a walk on Madison Avenue, like we used to. We started at Seventieth Street. We didn't hold hands, like the old days, but I swear he wore what must have been one of his beige bucket hats from **Annie Hall**. I had on my Marni dress, sans the Neptune Society letter from Tim Nicholson, over a black long-sleeved turtleneck and leggings, along with Prada boots, a big fat cross dangling around my neck, and the requisite wide-brimmed black hat. We looked in the windows of stores, starting with the Ralph Lauren complex on Seventy-second. We passed the Whitney. We took in the people. They took us in, as well. When we reached Campbell's mortuary, we looked at each other. He was seventy-seven. I was sixty-seven. Where did the time go? We walked into a corner deli, where he bought me a vanilla ice cream and a chocolate milk for himself.

Around Seventy-ninth Street, we ran into

Paul McCartney and his wife, Nancy. People gathered around us. It was almost like it used to be, only sweeter, because I knew it couldn't last. Paul waved goodbye as we headed back. I could almost hear Jimmy Durante sing, "Oh, it's a long, long while from May to December, but the days grow short when you reach September." We're there, Wood. We're in September. I didn't say it. He would have told me I was a dim-witted cretin and a worm to boot. I dropped him off at home, took a cab back to Grand Central Terminal, preserved for us by Jackie Kennedy, and rushed alongside fellow commuters to get on the train.

Every day I wake up, at least so far. Every day I wash my face in front of a mirror. And every day for the last few years I have a little chat with myself. "Okay, Diane . . . your hands still wash your face. You can still feel hot water. See's Candies peanut brittle is still your favorite dessert. The wild parrots on the telephone wire outside your bathroom still sing to you every morning, and just like them, you're still a live animal. Be grateful for what you have, you big jerk."

That said, it's still hard to wrap my mind around the fact that I'm a post–World War II demographic. I'm one of seventy-six million American children born between 1946 and 1964. That's right, I'm a baby boomer.

Major corporate boards require us to resign at sixty-five. Yet 42 percent of us are delaying retirement. Some 25 percent of us claim we'll never retire, and all of us refuse to acknowledge our coming demise. You can be sure that Steven Spielberg, Sly Stallone, and Rob Reiner at sixty-six; Goldie Hawn, Bette Midler, Steve Martin, and Cher at sixty-seven; sixty-eighty-year-old Michael Douglas; Joni Mitchell, Sam Shepard, and Robert De Niro at sixty-nine; David Geffen and Harrison Ford at seventy; Paul McCartney at seventy-one; Al Pacino at seventy-three; seventy-six-year-old Warren Beatty, Jack Nicholson, and Robert Redford; and, finally, seventy-seven-year-old Woody Allen are not retiring. Who cares if the U.S. government has proclaimed us old? We're not letting go. This past year the Social Security Administration informed me that my retirement age was sixty-six. I tell myself not to feel bad because my life expectancy is eighty-six, which means I have nineteen more years of life. I'll tell you one thing: I'm going to try to make the best of those nineteen years.

After all, I'm part of a group of seventy-five million American baby boomers who are in the beginning stages of learning how to let go.

The requirements for a good ending are difficult, considering my life choice. I'm a performer who chose my profession because I wanted to be loved by large groups of people. This sort of choice— actually, more an impulse than a choice—has led me here, right where I am today. On the way, I've learned to recognize beauty in the lives of role models like Dave Gold, the hardworking family guy who loved an idea and lived it. I respect the pigheaded courage of my money-mad grandmother Mary Hall. She did not leave this world afraid. I loved Grace Johansen for living out her dream, even if it didn't land her a star on the Hollywood Walk of Fame. My conversion from crush to friendship with Jack Nicholson has made me enjoy the company of men as friends, rather than hoped-for conquests. I live with a newfound respect and mourning for the dead I've lost, including Jackie Kennedy, who saved Grand Central Terminal so that years later people like me could walk inside its beauty and feel the thrill of art built in the name of transportation. As for Woody, the man who gave me this future, I am full of love. Without him, there would have been no senior ticket to Grand Central for me, no walk across newly refurbished Central Park, no pondering Grace in front of **A Beautiful Way to Go,** no Ricky Lauren, no Frank Zimmerman, no Dave Gold, and no dear Kathryn, either. All of it came to be because Woody Allen cast an unknown Diane Keaton for his play **Play It Again, Sam** in 1969 and then cast her in the movie version of **Play It Again, Sam,** followed by **Sleeper**, leading to **Annie Hall,** which sealed the deal for Diane Keaton.

These people, including and because of Woody, are my mentors, my heroes in the face of what hopefully will be a long, fascinating, new, and ever evolving journey to the great unknown. It's ironic, isn't it? I was never a fan of gold. I've never owned a gold watch or enjoyed looking at gold-leaf details on buildings or even church altars. I passed on gold gowns with gold accessories for the red carpet. "The golden years" is my least favorite metaphor for the period of life I'm living in. I have no interest in espousing the golden age of movies. I can't stand CNN's endless retirement commercials where two attractive elderly people smile at each other as they hold hands while walking into a soothing landscape, as if to say, **It's so peaceful accepting the autumn of life.** Golden oldies. The golden rule. A heart of gold. Worth its weight in gold. Gold shmold. The one saying that resonates through example, the one that has heart, the one that's worth its weight in gold is simple and true: Old is gold.

IN ONE EAR AND OUT THE OTHER

It seemed like an ordinary morning. I heard the water splash in the sink. Emmie barked as I washed my face. I rushed downstairs to the Nespresso machine. I heard the pod puncture. The sound of hot coffee hitting the bottom of my favorite glass. I took the first sip, and I heard my throat swallow. The glass cup clinking on the tile counter gave me a chill, and for the first time in my life, I wondered why I take sound for granted.

I've never considered the shape of my ears with any real interest. On occasion I put my finger in one only to feel the gnarly protrusions that lead to a dead end. That's usually when Spock comes to mind, or Dumbo, the flying elephant, or Prince Charles and, I'm sorry to say, Michael Phelps, too. That's when I remember Mom's best friend, Willie, telling me that Bing Crosby's ears were so big they had to be glued down. So much for the look of ears.

Listening doesn't seem connected to ears. Listening reverberates from ideas that have no concrete existence. Listening requires attention. I'm very good at hearing things I want to hear, like Duke's rant this morning about TLC's **My Strange Addiction,** perhaps the most disturbing reality show on television: "Mom. Last night I saw a woman eat rocks, a man who eats drywall . . . But wait, wait, wait, Mom, the best was the fat man who buys Ring Dings from the 7-Eleven, then pours gobs of tartar sauce over the chocolate topping, takes another Ring Ding, crushes them together like a sandwich, and eats them. Disgusting. Right, Mom? He's like really addicted to tartar sauce, right. But wait, Mom, the worst gross-out was the woman who drinks bleach every day and takes baths in it, too."

"Interesting, Duke, but I highly doubt she drinks it. Wouldn't she be dead if she drank bleach?"

Duke's observations are always entertaining. On the other hand, the nightmare of listening to four-year-old Duke screaming "MOM, MOM, MOM, MOM, MOM, MOM, MOM, MOM" at the top of his lungs, had been the kind of torment that made me want to rip out my hair.

Actually, I've heard there are forms of torture that render the slightest sound so unbearably loud, suicide seems the only relief. Not only have shrill sounds of wailing creatures been used to get information from prisoners. But some of the incarcerated have been tortured mercilessly by so-called "sound bombs." In Guantánamo Bay, Neil Diamond's "America" and Bruce Springsteen's "Born in the U.S.A." were used successfully. The euphemism for musical torture is called "acoustic bombardment."

One day a few years ago, a mild form of acoustic bombardment drove me nuts at breakfast. I suggested that Duke try not to turn the TV and radio on at the same time. Perhaps, I added, he shouldn't give his tutor, Russell O'Connell, a hard time after school every day as well. Dexter, not a morning person, yelled, "Mom, Duke came into my room without asking, jumped on the bed, and woke me up at six A.M."

"That's so not true, Dexter," Duke yelled back. "Oh, and P.S., Mom. Guess what? Russell O'Connell said you're impatient."

Wait one little minute—was I hearing right? Where did Russell O'Connell get off criticizing me in front of my son, especially since I happen to be his employer? Hurrying past Dexter, I got another update: "Mom, Duke fed the rats more cheese. They're so fat they're going to explode. What are you going to do about it?"

"Okay, okay, Dex. Just calm down. I'll take care of it."

Inside my bedroom, I shut the door and called Russell O'Connell. In no uncertain terms, I told him I didn't think it was a good idea to speak poorly of me to Duke, who, as we both knew, had issues with authority. Not deterred, Russell began a long-winded defense. Downstairs, I could hear the drama escalating. Cutting to the chase, I said, "Excuse me, Russell, with all due respect, just promise me you won't do that again." The clamor downstairs was getting out of hand. Miley Cyrus was singing at full volume, our neighbor's cat was howling in heat, Duke and Dexter were in a knock-down, drag-out fight, and Emmie was barking her head off at J.J., the gardener, who was collecting trash barrels. The sensory overload hit me like a stun gun, and suddenly, go figure, I knew what it must have felt like to be Russell O'Connell listening to me, Diane, mother of Duke, interrupting him yet again. That's when the truth came trumpeting in, and it was an unpleasant truth, an awful truth. Russell O'Connell was right: I **was** impatient.

In the car a half hour later, with Dexter driving, we set out for the bus stop. I turned on the radio. It was Rihanna with "Stay." Duke, sitting in the back, wanted to change the station to 97.1 AMP Radio. And me? I wanted Sirius radio's CNN with Carol Costello or NPR's **Morning Edition**. We flipped a coin. Duke won. AMP Radio played Skrillex's "Bangarang."

Music is too intense for everyday life. Take speakers. Why are speakers in so many rooms of so many houses? Speakers invite distraction. Sure, people love them, sure realtors recommend them for resale, but does anyone really want to live twenty-four/seven in Melody Land? It's inhumane. Music is not something you want invading your life when you're just trying to get through the day. Besides, built-in speakers look like giant ears sticking out of the walls.

At Sunset and Mandeville, Dexter interrupted my train of thought by asking if she could play Frank Ocean's new mixtape. "Sure, but slow down and pay attention to the signs. Okay, Dex? We're in a school zone." Ocean sang, "There will be tears I've no doubt. There may be smiles but a few." Tears, yeah, no doubt, I thought. "And when those tears have run out you will be numb and blue." Boy, that's for sure.

It was quiet in the car. Even Duke was silent. We all listened: "I can't be there with you, but I can dream. I can't be there with you, but I can dream. I still dream, dream, dream. I still dream." What is it about music? With the very first word of the first sentence, a song can hit you like a ton of bricks. It can reduce you to tears. It can part the sea. Music is the only experience that involuntarily illuminates our deepest feelings. Granted, what does it for me might not do it for you. But that doesn't change the fact that music is the most intoxicating of all the beauties combined, and it belongs to everyone.

Knowing that an emotional display was the last thing Dex could handle, I turned my head away and let the tears fall. Inside the window of Leoni's Laundr O Mat, I saw a woman smoking a cigarette as she folded clothes. "I can't be there with you, but I can dream." Was she dreaming? Was Dexter dreaming, too? Was she dreaming of Nico, her new boyfriend? Was there a smile as she thought of him, or a tear? "I can't be there with you. But I can dream."

I used to watch Mom put the needle down on a brand-new 33⅓ record album. Suddenly Bing Crosby's voice resonated through the living room while we opened Christmas presents. Music was a shared event. Mom would take out her sheet music and play the piano while Dorrie, Randy, Robin, and I practiced "Silent Night" before putting on our red wool scarves in Southern California's eighty-degree heat to go Christmas caroling. I can't remember a time I wasn't a member of a choir. Choirs were like being part of something larger than myself, something worthy of God. At Willard Junior High School, I was an alto with the all-girl Melodettes. We sang songs like "When the Red, Red Robin Comes Bob, Bob Bobbin' Along." The lyrics reminded me to be nicer to my sister Robin, even though she wasn't a bird, and she constantly stole the Hydrox cookies on my plate when Mom wasn't looking. In my senior year at Santa Ana High School, I was invited to join Harlan Anderson's Esquires and Debutantes, where we sang "You'll Never Walk Alone" in venues like the local Kiwanis Club. I never failed to cry. My tears were audience pleasers. Soon after, Mr. Anderson gave me my first solo. During the early 1970s, Joni Mitchell's "A Case of You" told me the story I wanted to hate but loved to hear. The story of goodbye. The perfect goodbye. The perfect loss. The perfect ache. Nothing does words better than music. . . . Joni was my first Frank Ocean. "I remember that time you told me, you said, 'Love is touching souls.' Surely you touched mine."

Dad's words were not like music when he used to say, "Diane, are you listening? Did you hear what I said? What did I say? You didn't listen, did you? How often do I have to tell you to close your mouth and open your ears?" This lecture always culminated with "In one ear and out the other, Diane. In one ear and out the other." Poor Dad—his advice invariably fell on deaf ears.

I was thinking about Dad's plight as Dexter pulled into the Arco gas station across the street from her bus stop. As I've gotten older, I'm proud to say, I've stopped being a selective listener, at least when it comes to Duke and Dexter. I'm their mother. I have to listen. But I want to, as well. "Mom. Mom."

"What, Duke?"

"Listen to this, and tell me what you think. Is it as good as Jason Lee or not? Listen. 'My name is Earl, and I'm just trying to be a better person.'"

"You got it down, bud, you got it down."

"Can I buy a pack of iD spearmint gum? Please?"

I gave him my credit card and told him to fill up the Rover and not to forget to get Dexter a pack, too. Dexter sighed. She was worried about the psychology test she'd taken. "There was a section where I had to know the hypothesis, the subjects, the control group, the experimental group, the independent and dependent variables, and the results for two experiments we learned. If I got four wrong, Ms. Kopick will pretty much probably give me a low C or a high

D. I knew the experiments, but I'm pretty sure my hypothesis was wrong."

Duke came back as Dexter's bus arrived. Before I knew it, she was out the door, and gone. But wait a minute, what was the result? Was it C bad or D bad? "Mom, how's this? Miiiiyyy naahemm is Errrrrrrrrrllll. And Iey'mmmm jeest tryin to beeeee a better peeeerson." Me too, Duke.

After I dropped Duke off, I turned the radio to 89.3 and I heard Gregg Korbon begin to tell his wife, Kathryn, a story. I was familiar with StoryCorps's recordings of ordinary Americans on NPR. I lingered on the word "ordinary" and started to listen.

There's a Little League baseball field in Charlottesville called Brian C. Korbon Field, and I would like to tell the story of how it got its name. The story goes back twelve years ago, when our son Brian was getting ready for his ninth birthday in January. He started having difficulties sleeping and he said that he did not want to celebrate his birthday. He said celebrating his birthday would bring his death and he would never make it to double digits, meaning ten years old. We didn't understand that, because he was healthy. He had had heart surgery when he was a little baby, but that had gone well, and the doctors told us that we really didn't have anything to worry about. . . . His mother would cuddle him at night and talk to him about his fears—he had terrific fears about going to sleep. And we had a child psychologist see him, because we couldn't understand why he had these fears.

Well, over the next several months he got better, and he seemed to be coming out of his depression. He started to say he wanted to have a party—his belated birthday party—but he didn't want it to be called a birthday party. He wanted it to be called a Happy Spring party, so we planned it, and he wanted to just have three friends. He had a friend named Ben, a little girlfriend named Jamie, and he had a boy named Cam that had always wanted to be friends with him, but Brian didn't really spend much time with them. It was kind of like he was trying to finish up unfinished business.

Now, during the two weeks before the party, Brian did lots of unusual things. He got Kathryn's Mother's Day card in advance and a present. Mother's Day was two weeks away. And then he also got my Father's Day present, even though that was months away. He got a trophy he picked out that said "World's Greatest Dad," and he begged Kathryn to get it, but she said, "It's a couple months away. We don't have to do that yet." He wrote letters to his grandparents—all the things that he'd been planning to do and hadn't done, and his spirit seemed to be getting much better. . . .

The morning of his birthday party he woke up and there were several things he did down in his room that we didn't realize till later, but he wrote letters to some of his friends and put a sign on his door. The sign said, "On a trip. Don't worry about me." And then the kids came for the party, and they had a great little party. He didn't want any gifts, but his little girlfriend gave him a kiss and his friend Ben wrote a song for him. And then it was time for them to leave and for Brian to play Little League. He'd just joined this team. He wasn't very good. He was the littlest kid on the team. I took him, and Kathryn was going to join us a little bit later. . . .

We went to the baseball field. When Brian got there, he was so brave. He had always been afraid of the ball and kind of tried to shrink away from ground balls and stuff like that. But he was fearless. He was charging after the ground balls and he was really just having the best time. He had said he wanted to score a run more than anything. So I was sitting in the stands and it was his first time up at bat. He got walked to first base. The next little boy hit a triple, and Brian ran around the bases, crossed home plate. This was his second game, and the last time he got stranded at third base and didn't make it home. So this time he tore around the bases, crossed home plate, and the fans gave him a big applause, and he looked up at the stands and our eyes met, and he was the happiest little boy you ever saw.

He gave me a high five and went into the dugout. And then he collapsed. And the coach brought him out—his limp body out—and I looked at him, and he was blue. And I'm an anesthesiologist, and that's what I do, is resuscitate people, and I resuscitated him. But something inside told me he wasn't coming back. The ambulance came, which was right across the street, and we went to the hospital with him. They tried to resuscitate him, and he wouldn't come back.

After he died, I went to the ballfield to get my car, and it was the most beautiful spring day I have ever seen—the next day was Mother's Day. The honeysuckle was out, which for that early in the year is very unusual, and there was another Little League game playing and barbecues going on with square dancing in the picnic shelters around the field. And I was standing in the field looking at the other kids playing, and I smelled the honeysuckle, and the clouds were beautiful—crisp, blue sky. . . . Then all of a sudden, everything got very clear. I've since heard other people describe this kind of great moment—that I could see everything clearer than I'd ever seen. The colors were clearer and brighter and the smells were stronger, and I had the sense that everything was okay. I was at peace. And that, if I could bring Brian back, it would be for me, not for him—that he had finished. He had finished his job here, and the unfinished business was just mine.

I've never known a "great moment," or the sudden awareness of everything becoming crystal clear. I've never experienced a devastating tragedy. But I heard Gregg's words. I listened. His story entered my thoughts through the sound of his voice in my ears. It was unlike other perceptions of beauty, which in my case usually come with the word NEED. Hearing Gregg did not make me try to one-up him with my own tale of woe. There was no thought of casting myself in his story, as if I could somehow make it mine, as if I were the narrator. This wasn't like listening to music. It was more like an act of love. And, like love, it came with a price. Contrary to what I'd always thought, being an audience is active. If you want to be an active listener, it's best to say one thing, and one thing only, and that is this: "What happened next?"

The day turned out to be anything but ordinary. School was over. The kids were back home. It was almost dinnertime. Duke was mastering his "I'm just trying to be a better person." Dex was taking selfies on her iPhone. I forged my way to the treadmill in the basement. The new house has speakers in every room. I turned the treadmill to 45, almost a jog, and started learning lines from the movie I was about to make back east. As my character, Leah, I was saying, "Sometimes life outlives love. After Eugene died, I never thought I would love again, but—" when I suddenly heard No Doubt's "Don't Speak" blasting all the way from the kitchen.

I tried to keep my mouth shut. But a few minutes later, subjected to the sound of Flo Rida rapping, "If you like my body, touch me, touch me, touch me, touch me, touch me," I'd had it. That was it. "Turn it off! Dexxxxxter, turn it off. NOW!" No response. I got off the treadmill and ran to the stairs. "DEXTER. Did you hear me?" No response. The sound of talking made me pause. It was Dexter and my friend Lindsay. They seemed to be having a good time. Then Duke joined in, too. Then I heard them laugh. After that, the floor started vibrating with the sound of feet moving, and I heard more laughter. I guess the point is, how will I know if I like or dislike a sound, much less a song, if I refuse to hear it? How will I experience Gregg Korbon's story if I don't turn up the volume and listen? I've been called impatient by Russell O'Connell, the tutor, but he wasn't wrong. He was right. And that's when I said to myself, "Let it go, Diane. Let them go." And I did, I let them go.

HEALING HUMOR

I was speaking to the graduating sixth-grade class at UCLA Lab School. My speech included a brief appreciation of the school's acclaimed research and innovation in children's education. It seemed to be going well when I mentioned how honored we were to have UCLA's chancellor, Gene Block, at our gathering. Marc Shaiman, my accompanist, started riffing on the piano. I took his cue and began to sing "God Bless America." I heard a couple of boos. Out of the corner of my eye, I saw a few people, including Dr. Block and his wife, Carol, leave. Apparently "God Bless America" was the wrong choice for our progressive elementary school community. Others stood up and left as well. Mortified, I was barely able to get through the song.

Afterward, as soon as I reached the car, I called Carol Kane, crying. She was in the middle of a meeting with potential backers for her one-woman show on Bette Davis and didn't have time to talk. Later, at the Grill in Beverly Hills, I ran into Warren Beatty. Why hadn't he thanked me for the speech I gave at his AFI tribute two years ago? I knew I was no Elaine May, but still, a word of gratitude? I excused myself and went to the bathroom, where there was no toilet paper. Worse, the toilet wouldn't flush. I tried to clean up the mess with my hands, but the water in the bowl started rising, and so did everything else. I ran to the sink, grabbed several paper towels, and found Hillary Clinton dancing with a naked man in the stall next to mine. A loud noise terrified me. I woke up screaming. The burglar alarm was going off.

"MOM! MOM!" Duke ran into the room. "I'm scared, Mom."

"I know, don't worry, Duke. Don't worry." He grabbed my hand as we rushed to the panel in the hallway. When I looked to see which room had triggered the alarm, there was no explanation. Squeezing my hand, Duke said, "Did you hear that, Mom?"

"Hear what?"

"The noise coming from the kitchen?"

"There's no noise in the kitchen, Duke. Trust me, we're fine."

After checking all the windows with steak knives in our hands, just in case, we still hadn't heard from the alarm company. Where was the call within thirty seconds? Where was the concerned voice at the other end of the line reassuring us the police would come? What's the point of having an alarm if no one calls? Screw that.

It was three forty-five in the morning. Duke was still convinced that hooded men with assault weapons were lurking in some dark corner. So I broke the cardinal rule and let him get into bed with Emmie and me. It was a matter of life and death, right?

An hour later, I woke up to another alarm. I looked over at my clock. It wasn't the crickets chirping on my iPhone. It was an Amber Alert from San Diego. The suspect, a Caucasian male, was believed to be traveling to Texas or Canada with a sixteen-year-old girl. Goddamnit. Life was a nightmare. I couldn't get back to sleep.

At five-thirty, Duke woke up asking if he could watch **Jackass** on Apple TV. "Go back to sleep, Duke."

"You know what you are, Mom?" he laughed. "You're a creepy-ass cracker, like that little fat girl said on TV at the trial where the man killed a boy in a hoodie."

"I don't think it's a good idea to call your mother a creepy-ass cracker, or anyone else, for that matter, and NO you cannot watch **Jackass**. It's time to go back to sleep."

"I'm awake. Could you make French toast for breakfast, with sliced strawberries, too?"

"Okay. Okay. All right, but the deal is, you have to get ready for school. Got it?"

Then it was time to wake up Dexter. Never a treat. I wasn't surprised that she'd slept through both alarms. In 2008, she'd slept through the 5.4 Chino Hills earthquake. "Dexter. You have to get up." No response. "Dexter, now." No response. Forget it. I went downstairs, fed Duke, fed Emmie, and was washing the dishes when she sauntered in, speechless, fifteen minutes later. "Are you angry about something?" I asked.

"Mom, I'm not a morning person!!!" And with that she took the keys and left.

"Duke. Let's go. I'll be in the car," I yelled. Taking his cue from Dexter, he opened the door, turned the seat warmer on even though it was September, and dropped his buttered French toast onto my favorite bowler hat on the floor. "Hey, Mom. Listen to this: Mom puts the eek in cheek, the why in my eye, and, best of all, the dart in my fart. Like it?"

"It's great, Duke."

This was fast shaping up to be the worst day ever. Okay, okay, overexaggeration. At least it was a Friday, I was thinking, and I could sleep in tomorrow, when suddenly the crickets summoned. It was Dexter in tears. She'd rear-ended a truck on the Pacific Coast Highway. I put the pedal to the metal and hit Temescal as fast as I could before hopping onto the highway. Even though Duke was wearing headphones, I heard Robin Thicke's "Blurred Lines" coming through loud and clear. "Let me be the one you back that ass to." Thanks, Robin.

After I took care of Dexter's tears, and the angry woman's ruined bumper, I wondered why Hillary Clinton had danced with a naked man in a bathroom stall. Dreams can be deranged. But life is a journey that seems to be going nowhere. There was no beauty to be found in its absurdity. There was no beauty, period. Why did I have to be over the hill, anxious, frustrated, overwrought, and bumbling? It was eight A.M. Goddamnit. I was exhausted. I needed help. And therapy wouldn't do it, because of course, I'd been therapized, acupuncturized, analyzed, hypnotized, and yogatized enough for one inconsequential woman on the verge of a nervous breakdown.

As soon as I got home, I decided to try the

advice of Dr. Tan, my acupuncturist, and take a backward walk with Emmie in an effort to employ the unutilized part of my brain. According to Dr. Tan, this would help ward off future dementia. A person's got to keep trying. That's what I said to myself. So I straightened my shoulders, grabbed Emmie's leash, and, barefoot, began to walk backward from my house to the bluff. Goodbye, house; goodbye, giant sycamore tree; goodbye, Wynola Street.

I'm not a fan of goodbyes. I began to worry. I couldn't see what was approaching. Was I close to the bluff? Would I fall off? All of a sudden I heard my neighbor Dolores say, "Hello, Diane." As I turned my head and looked up, I tripped over a rock, fell down, and broke my toe. Immediately, I started screaming, "I hate you. I hate you, you fucking toe. Fuck you!" Was I crazy? It wasn't my toe's fault; I'd already broken four. But, come on, this was the last thing I needed. Especially when I knew my podiatrist would scold me for walking backward barefoot. To hell with it. I didn't care; I'm not going to wear shoes every second of every day for the rest of my life. It's one of the few remaining sensory pleasures I have, goddamnit.

After a half hour of waiting in pain at the doctor's office, I went on Pinterest. My obsession. My love. On Sarah Smith's board I found a photograph of Vanessa Paradis's gap-toothed smile and pinned it. It made me remember Lauren Hutton. I recalled sitting in the front row of Warren Robertson's acting class in midtown Manhattan watching Lauren Hutton walk onto the stage after James Earl Jones had given an acting exercise. I could tell she was nervous. Nothing particularly stuck out from her monologue, until she made a mistake and unashamedly smiled. That's when I saw the big black hole between her two front teeth.

Now it's different. Gaps are cool. But not all gaps are equal. Mick Jagger's Georgia May has a smile that's a sexy anomaly, like Vanessa Paradis's. Lauren Hutton's beamed from the depth of a glorious flaw. The flaw was its perfection. I've seen a lot of smiles and I've dished out my fair share, but Lauren Hutton's smile, while enviable, did not make me envious. I didn't try to steal it for myself. I recognized it as a transforming gift she'd been given. It made me want to spread the joy, and pay it forward.

Jessica Lange keeps her smile close. That's its brilliance. Who will ever forget Julia Roberts's megawatt grin in **Pretty Woman**? Ryan Gosling's is small but dangerously effective on women. What about the before-and-after effect of Barack Obama's smile? You may say I'm off my rocker, but hear me out: President Obama is a man with two faces. I would venture to say no face has ever been more transformed by a smile. Every American has seen President Obama's face bear the weight of disappointing setbacks. And every American has seen it mutate instantaneously from solemn into a kind of jubilation brimming with empathy and the humility only a great man can project. President Obama's smile is an anomaly we'll never see again.

I remembered Grammy Keaton saying, "There's an Irish colleen sitting on your face waiting to reveal herself by turning up the ends of your pretty little mouth. Smile, Diane." I took her advice and learned that my smile was a multiservice instrument. It could express pleasure, sociability, and amusement, too. I began to understand that "service with a smile" could be a way of life. One of my first jobs was behind the candy counter at the Broadway Theater in Santa Ana, California. I smiled more than any of my fellow workers, and I noticed that people liked being treated cordially.

While waiting in the reception area with my broken toe, I had an epiphany. Maybe my smile could help me make it through the day. Maybe I could stop being so aggravated if I wore a smile.

Back in the car after my appointment with the podiatrist, I got a call from Sandra, reminding me that I'd promised Duke and his friends Jackson,

Zeke, Ben, Atticus, and Core that I'd take them to see **Grown Ups 2**. What? Sorry, I told her, but I had to bow out. The last thing I needed to do was buy popcorn for six male tweens and go see an hour and a half of fart jokes.

Then Stephanie called and asked me if I wanted the good news first or the bad. Thanks, Stephanie. That was the exact moment when the police car's siren pulled me over on Roxbury. I sat in the car with my throbbing toe as the officer informed me I'd been holding the phone to my ear while driving. Did I know it was against the law? Giving my new method a try, I smiled. Apparently, he was not charmed. I gave him my friendly "Sorry, I'll never do it again" smile, another try. I even complimented him on his mustache. And you know what he did? He handed me the ticket without comment and drove away. So much for Charlie Chaplin, the little tramp, and his "You'll find that life is still worthwhile if you just smile."

It was five in the evening. Oh, and did I mention that the boys, all of them, were going to spend the night, too? I was late. The movie started at six. My toe was killing me. I was speeding and screaming at drivers, especially those who respected the speed limit. I got home at five forty-five, grabbed the boys from Sandra, piled them into the car, and headed to the AMC in

Santa Monica. I could barely keep my anger inside. With no time to buy popcorn, we ran into the theater at the end of the credits.

Grown Ups 2 opened with a frightened elk inside Adam Sandler's bedroom urinating about six gallons of piss all over Sandler's face. Okay, the guys started howling. And me? I couldn't help but laugh, too. I knew it was juvenile. But it felt good. When Kevin James was forced to cliff-dive naked into a lake and landed testicles first on the head of David Spade, who made some rude joke about being trapped inside Kevin James's asshole, we all laughed, me included. When Richie Minervini, as "Principal Tardio," an overweight man in a belly-exposing T-shirt, pulled a Froot Loop out of his navel and ate it, I was howling with the boys. It was the best thing to happen all day. The movie was awful, as in awful funny. Belly-laugh funny. And the audience agreed. When David Spade's character found himself accidentally pushed inside a monster truck–sized tire, which then rolled down a hill until it bounced off Shaquille O'Neal and fell onto its side, making Spade vomit fifteen feet across the road onto a nearby police officer who looked exactly like the cop who gave me the ticket, that's when I laughed louder than anyone in the theater.

I'm not the only one who loves a pratfall served with slapstick humiliation. It's called low comedy. Low comedy is looked down upon because it's targeted toward people who want to feel better by laughing at someone else's misery. Obviously it's not respected among certain circles, and yet comic geniuses like Buster Keaton, the Three Stooges, Laurel and Hardy, Steve Martin, Martin Short, Jerry Lewis, and Jim Carrey are some of its masters. To me, sight gags are as intellectually challenging to pull off as a pun. Watch the setup to a great pratfall, and you'll see the tension build to some form of physical gag that releases it, and BOOM . . . that's where the laugh comes in. No one has to feel guilty, or apologize for laughing at Adam Sandler's misfortune, in the safety of a theater. In fact, it makes us, the audience, feel better about our own trials and tribulations.

Melissa McCarthy may be the first female low-comedy genius in film. She can do anything, say anything, and get away with it. She's a foulmouthed truck-driving ball breaker who can dish it out with the rest of the guys. The difference is, she can also make you cry on a dime. That's the female in her. She's vulnerable. But in **The Heat,** when Captain Frank Woods says to her, "You look like one of the Campbell Soup kids who grew up to be an alcoholic" and she says, "That's a misrepresentation of my vagina"—come on. That's funny. I know, 'cause I'm laughing just writing it down. The Women in Film organization should stand up and applaud Kristen Wiig, too. Only in **Bridesmaids** do the gals get to be the gals **and** the guys as well. Bring it on, Melissa and Kristen. The world is theirs. **Bridesmaids** was groundbreaking. Take the scene where Kristen Wiig, playing Annie, is about to have a meltdown when she's confronted by a snotty teenage girl at the jewelry store she works at. The girl walks in and stares at Kristen.

13-YEAR-OLD GIRL: You're weird.

ANNIE: I'm not weird. OK?

13-YEAR-OLD GIRL: Yes, you are.

ANNIE: No, I'm not! And you started it.

13-YEAR-OLD GIRL: No, you started it! Did you forget to take your Xanax this morning?

ANNIE: Oh, I feel bad for your parents.

13-YEAR-OLD GIRL: I feel bad for your face.

ANNIE: OK . . . well, call me when your boobs come in.

13-YEAR-OLD GIRL: You call me when yours come in.

ANNIE: What do you have, four boyfriends?

13-YEAR-OLD GIRL: Exactly.

ANNIE: OK . . . yeah, have fun having a baby at your prom.

13-YEAR-OLD GIRL: You look like an old mop.

ANNIE: You know, you're not as popular as
you think you are.

13-YEAR-OLD GIRL: I am very popular.

ANNIE: (sticks tongue in cheek and mimics
fellatio) Oh, I'm sure you are . . . very . . .
popular.

13-YEAR-OLD GIRL: Well, you're an old
single loser who's never going to have any
friends.

ANNIE: You're a little cunt!

Unlike Kristin and Melissa, when it comes
to comedy, I've mostly played sidekick half-
wits. In **Annie Hall** I was elevated to the role
of an inarticulate young woman who wanted to
mold herself into someone more sophisticated.
Duh!!! Inarticulate! Awkward?! It was a walk
in the park. With **Baby Boom,** Charles Shyer
and Nancy Meyers gave me the role of cracker-
jack businesswoman J. C. Wiatt, a woman who
needed to be taken down a couple of notches
by a baby in order to triumph. It was more of a
stretch to pull off. I guess you could say it was
my attempt to enter the lofty world of high comedy, characterized by witty dialogue and biting
humor.

Sleeper and **Love and Death,** two early
Woody Allen movies, were a lot of fun. It was
second nature for me to play birdbrains and

spoiled brats. Woody's humor in those movies revolved around sex, a bodily function that
leads to a release, just like laughter. So were these
movies low comedy, or did the witty dialogue
set them apart? In **Sleeper** my character, Luna,
asks Woody's character, Miles, if he would like to
perform sex.

MILES: Perform sex? Uh, uh, I don't think
    I'm up to a performance, but I'll rehearse
    with you, if you like.
LUNA: Okay. I just thought you might want
    to; they have a machine here.
MILES: Machine? I'm not getting into that
    thing. I, I'm strictly a hand operator; you
    know, I, I . . . I don't like anything with
    moving parts that are not my own.

Later in the movie Luna says, "It's hard to believe that you haven't had sex for two hundred
years." Miles responds with, "Two hundred four,
if you count my marriage."

In **Love and Death,** my character, Sonja,
complains to Boris (Woody) that she's unhappy.

BORIS: Oh, I wish you weren't.
SONJA: Voskovec and I quarrel frequently.
    I've become a scandal.
BORIS: Poor Sonja.

SONJA: For the past weeks, I've visited
   Seretski in his room.
BORIS: Why? What's in his room? Oh!!
SONJA: And before Seretski, Aleksei, and
   before Aleksei, Alegorian, and before
   Alegorian, Asimov, and—
BORIS: OKAY!!!
SONJA: Wait, I'm still on the A's.
BORIS: How many lovers do you have?
SONJA: In the midtown area?

It's true, both **Love and Death** and **Sleeper**
were set in worlds where complex situations
were hashed over among articulate people. But
the primary topic, sex, was delivered by a couple
of dimwits. Did that make Woody's early movies high or low comedy? Does anyone care? Not
really. And anyway, comedy is not a science. It's
an art. As soon as you try to analyze it, the fun-
niness disappears. All I can say is, I wish I had
made more comedies.

On the drive home, I forgot about my throbbing toe. I forgot I was a broken-down privileged
white woman of a certain age with a crabby attitude. What difference did it make if Chancellor Block and his wife had walked out on "God
Bless America" in a nightmare? Sure, the alarm
going off at three in the morning was worse than
the nightmare, any nightmare. Yes, Dexter was

annoying with her first fender bender. And, of course, I needed to work on Duke's creepy-ass cracker language skills. No, I had not been able to charm the police officer. Yes, I was the kind of idiot who chose to walk backward barefoot only to fall and break her toe for the fourth time. . . . But—and it's a big but—at the end of the day, I had to get down on my knees, praise the Lord, and thank **Grown Ups 2** for reversing a possible (and, I admit, self-imposed) mental breakdown with the quickest of fixes. Laughter. It had been a rough day. But wasn't it ironic that I would find myself in a theater watching a movie about grown-ups where the gag was that grown-ups were anything but grown-up?

None of this, not one bit, downgrades the beauty of a smile. Not at all. It's one thing to see a smile like Barack Obama's. It's another to feel it. A smile is appreciation, and empathy, and wonder. But laughter is release. Laughter is letting go. Babies laugh three hundred times a day. Adults twenty, if we're lucky. What is it with being an adult? Does growing up—and, in my case, growing old—have to be characterized by increased seriousness and less laughter? I intend to join the babies of the world and laugh more. Especially since—and this is a fact—laughter leads to less stress. It just does. So while smiling is lovely . . . laughing is beautiful.

IN LOVE WITH THE NIGHT

I appeared to be a nice girl. I obeyed my mother, who said, "Diane is a lot of fun to be with. She does her chores without any complaints." I had a sun-filled life. Our family vacations took us to national parks like Yosemite and Bryce Canyon. We went to drive-in theaters and saw movies like **Seven Brides for Seven Brothers.** I sang in the church choirs and ate Cheerios for breakfast. I was an innocent girl living in Southern California when the specter of starless nights came calling.

I can't pinpoint when dark became beautiful. At first it was shadows hiding bloodthirsty ghouls, who would break into our home by smashing the windows with mallets and then kill us all. Dark was the sound of rats scrabbling on the floor in the middle of the night, ready to leap into my bed and eat me alive. Dark meant something else, too. It meant tiptoeing into the kitchen after Mom and Dad were asleep to sneak a plateful of chocolate chip cookies. The only time to accomplish this "mission impossible" was in the quiet dark of Night.

I was ten years old on the day I flipped through the pages of **Life** magazine and found a photo-graph of Sophia Loren. She sat on a stack of newspapers wearing a bathing suit and a pair of black patent leather stilettos. Her face had a sul-try "take me" look. She was not sunny. There was something else, too. She appeared to have a long black line between her breasts. Later I learned that it had a name. Cleavage. Sophia Loren had lots of cleavage. I told no one of my new interest. Not Jesus in my prayers, or his father, God. Not Mom. Not Dad. No one. What I did was begin to hunt down other **Life** magazines, in search of more cleavage.

A year later, my cousin Charlie Rupert took me to see a matinee of the movie **Kiss Me Deadly**. It was about a serial killer who kissed his victims, put a gun to their heads, and pulled the trigger.

They were called women of the night. Like Sophia Loren, they had cleavage, but theirs jostled
around inside V-neck sweaters worn over tight
skirts. Later, Mom told me women of the night
were sad because they sold their bodies. I told
Mom I would never sell mine if it meant getting shot in the head. But I did want to know
what sort of services were provided in the body-
selling business. "Something not nice," Mom
said. "Something not nice."

Grammy Hall's fixation on the death of
Johnny Stompanato wasn't nice, either. One tabloid suggested that the movie star Lana Turner
found Mr. Stompanato in bed with her fourteen-
year-old daughter, Cheryl Crane. Distraught,
she grabbed a kitchen knife and stabbed him to
death. That was one story. The **Herald Examin-
er**'s was different. Cheryl heard screams, ran into
her mother's bedroom, saw Johnny Stompanato
choking her, rushed for a knife, and plunged it
into his heart. After a lengthy trial, the jury con-
victed Cheryl of justifiable homicide. She was
made a ward of the state of California and sent
to a home for problem girls; she escaped from
that home in 1960.

I'd never heard of a girl killing a man, or a man
in bed with a girl, or a movie star nearly choked
to death by a gigolo. The death of Johnny Stompanato was a Hollywood morality tale driven by a

fading movie star's unbalanced longing for a man of questionable character with swarthy appeal. At the center of the story was a teenage problem girl only two years older than me. Tabloid photographs showed an enigmatic Cheryl Crane being taken away in handcuffs. At Cheryl's age, I was not an enigma, or a murderess. But I did want something about me to be alluring, even dangerous. I wanted to wear black stockings with black seams. Anything with a hint of shadow. A black belt over a black skirt, a gunmetal-gray wallet with a midnight-blue change purse. You get the drift. I began to understand the beauty of a little light mixed with dark. You could have both. Black and white. Dark and light. Good times and bad. Pain with pleasure.

I was a junior in high school when Marilyn Monroe committed suicide. Somewhere in the darkest reaches of my mind, I understood that her breathless insecurity not only held the weight of her appeal but may have caused her death. My girlfriend Tammy said it was because she was getting old and her personal life wasn't so hot. Plus, she had no children. I wasn't so sure.

I lingered over a picture in the paper of a black-haired man clinging to his scrapbook as a tornado approached. Watching Channel 13's local news, I cried when I saw the broken Barbie doll a little girl grasped as the floodwaters rose.

They seemed to be holding on to mementos of the dreams they'd lost on the way. Were my dreams going to get lost, too? I knew that roses faded, but I didn't understand the thing about how when you reach "the peak of perfection" you also "begin to wither." I hadn't clocked in beauty as a "time's up" trick played on all of us.

By that time I had my very own cleavage and I was a high school musical comedy star, applauded in particular for my antics. Boys thought I was marriage material. Girls thought I was fun. But underneath my affable veneer, I was beginning to spread a little dark into my light. At Santa Ana Junior College, I smoked marijuana with my friend Leslie, in my dad's VW van. Was I bad? Were questionable choices overshadowing my lily-white reputation?

I was twenty-two when I landed a role in the Broadway production of **Hair**. As soon as it became a giant hit, the entire cast went on a trip to Fire Island and took peyote. Me included. I swallowed a pill called MDA with a young man I dated; he laughed when I told him I saw a witch fly across his face on a broom. A few seconds later, his eyes became thousands of crisscrossing spiderwebs. I stuck my finger in one and it disappeared into a wall of thick black goo. Was I compiling a mountain of ominous secrets that would reveal the real Diane?

I wasn't prepared for Al Pacino. We'd been cast in **The Godfather.** Neither of us had a clue that we were going to make a movie that would go on to be considered one of the greatest films in American cinema. Try to picture this: We met in a bar in New York. I was awkward, and Al? Al was as mysterious as the love I felt for him the moment I saw his face. I didn't want to be friendly—"Hi, I'm Diane"—or go through the "Nice to meet you, Diane" bit, either. There was nothing nice about my thoughts. His face, his nose, and what about those eyes? I kept trying to figure out what I could do to make them mine. They never were. That was the lure of Al. He was never mine. For the next twenty years I kept losing a man I'd never had. After Al, I began building a wall around my vulnerability. More hats. Long-sleeved everything. Coats in the summer. Boots with knee socks and wool suits with scarves at the beach. Woody said it best in a phone message: "I'm standing in front of your house, 820 Roxbury. It's very beautiful. I'd like to get in, but I don't have a hammer."

My friend Daniel Wolf advised me to "want what you have." Want what I have? Oh, Daniel. He didn't get it. Of all the beauties I've shared a bed with, Al's blacker-than-midnight version was unmatchable. Even before he quit the bottle,

Al was the kind of drinker who played out his nights at Joe Allen's bar reading Shakespeare to a group of like-minded actors. It was his love of language. It was the sound of his voice. It was his continuously evolving face. That was the miracle of his beauty. Evolution. As we got more familiar, I took every opportunity to make him marriage material. My project did not work. All my failed efforts only increased my obsession. What did I learn? Never fall in love with the Godfather. Never stumble over a dark knight with shadowy beauty and deep talent.

Eventually Al became a father to twins, with Beverly D'Angelo. In 2010 I was a mother to Duke, age nine, and Dexter, age fourteen. My movie **Morning Glory** was a failure at the box office, and Al Pacino was broke, or so it was suggested on the CNN interview I caught at my brother Randy's new home in the retirement community of Belmont Village. Maybe Al had been hit by the recession. Whatever it was, he seemed to have changed for the better. Maybe those twins of his made him happy. Was I jealous? I don't know; all I know is that as soon as I allowed myself to register those old feelings, I got queasy, and I threw up in Randy's bathroom. When I came out, Randy asked if I was pregnant. Pregnant in my mid-sixties? "Pregnant, Randy?"

I asked, dumbfounded. What world was he living in? The world of dreams? The world of phantasmagoric possibilities?

Not the world of another Diane; oh no, not in the world of Diane von Furstenberg and media mogul Barry Diller. You can be sure that Diane wasn't thinking about how to introduce the new version of her old black-and-white wrap dress when an interviewer said, "I think there's a lot of curiosity about your marriage to Barry Diller." This was her response: "I don't understand what there is to understand. This man has been my lover, my friend, and now he's my husband. I've been with him for thirty-five years. At times we were separated, at times we were only friends, at times we were lovers, at times we're husband and wife. That's our life." That's their life, but mine? I will never marry. Do I envy their ability to weather the storm and stick with the deal they struck? Yes. I do, but my love of the impossible far overshadowed the rewards of longevity. I fell for the beauty of a broken bird. The ecstasy of failure. It was the only marriage I could make with a man. Black with a little white. Pain mixed with pleasure.

Diana Vreeland was not born with less. She was born with more—more ugliness than most women in the world of fashion and beauty could bear. The black–as–Grecian Formula hair slicked behind her ears and the cigarette dangling from her cherry-red lips were mere background material for the schnozzola sitting stage center in the wreckage of a face that defied compliance. Early on, she must have figured it was better to embrace the bad news and go with it. That's exactly what she did. She paraded her flamboyant style while turning beauty toward the light of publication. As in the title of the documentary about her **The Eye Has to Travel,** her eyes traveled. They traveled when she worked at **Harper's Bazaar.** They traveled when she was editor in chief of **Vogue** magazine. When she established herself as the premiere curator for the Costume Institute of the Metropolitan Museum of Art, her eyes took her on trips that gave the public some of the most extraordinary exhibitions in the history of the Met.

Diana Vreeland was a walking, talking master class on beauty. She did not tighten her face. She did not lift it. She did not chop off her unsightly nose or pull up her failing neck. She was a woman in the precarious world of fashion who embellished her flaws with a religious zeal that made her beautiful. Her black hair was still lacquered when the "elegant Crane picking her way out of a swamp," as Cecil Beaton described her, died of a heart attack in her eighties.

I admired her gumption. Her face did not interfere with her mission. She was not swept up with regret. For Diana Vreeland, flaunting her flaws embellished the empire of beauty she created. I don't wear the truth on my face. I've hidden my dark side with a smile.

This summer, on the last day of filming **And So It Goes,** I shot the final scene by myself. Leah, a sixty-five-year-old wannabe lounge singer, had fallen in love with Oren, played by Michael Douglas. They'd flirted. They'd kissed. They'd had sex. Feeling pressured, Oren had abandoned Leah. To get back in her good graces, he'd managed to secure an audition for her at a nightclub called Victors. Leah had landed the job. They'd gotten closer. Leah felt hopeful, only to learn Oren had unexpectedly sold his house and was moving away.

The crew members were saying goodbye to each other as they set up the shot. The rest of the cast was gone, even Michael. I knew I had to break down, but I was filled with anxiety, and told Rob Reiner, the director. He shrugged his shoulders. What could he do? It was my job. Before "Action" he had one direction: "Cry."

Suddenly I was sitting on a bar stool at Victors, speaking into a microphone: "The next song has a special meaning for me. I was seventeen, and this song was playing when I realized I was in love for the first time. That first time is so powerful you can't imagine ever having those feelings for anyone else. But sometimes life outlives love. I never thought I'd love again, but here I am, still singing this song, still dreaming of love." With that I nodded to my accompanist, played by Rob, and began singing: "The shadow of your smile when you are gone will color all my dreams and light the dawn." When I got to "Our wistful little star was far too high. A tear-drop kissed your lips and so did I," I forgot I was making a movie in Stamford, Connecticut. I forgot the camera was pushing in on my face. I forgot about the audience of extras feigning interest, and I don't know why, but I began to cry. "Now when I remember spring, and all the joy that love can bring, I will be remembering the shadow of your smile." Only later did I realize that it was the music that had affected me. It was the recognition that sometimes life does outlive love. It was the regret of thinking I'd never love again, or see the color of my dreams light the dawn, but it was also knowing that in spite of everything, to still be singing a song, and still dreaming of love, was enough for me.

My father and mother lived with the dream of love for fifty years. It didn't matter how often the army of darkness approached. When Dad was dying, he still sang his song to Mom. He sang it from the mystery of his journey. Mom wrote it down. I found what she wrote about it. I wrote that down, too.

"We took a shower together on Sunday. We both had a feeling of closeness even though he was not the same. I scrubbed him good, and washed his hair. We kissed and hugged for a long time and said tender things to one another. I got to feel his body which I've loved for so many years. I'll never forget these moments we have together. The grasping for one another's hand; the squeeze. The long looks, he with his good eye, I with my owl glasses bumping him in the face as I lean in to kiss him. Tonight our kisses were long and open; our special kind. Our intimacy was the same as it was when we first met, forty-seven years ago. I told him about when I saw him at the door for our first date. His eyes were risky, direct, and light blue. I loved his eyes from the first moment I looked at him. As I held on tight with a long gaze, Jack told me he was climbing down off the ladder of steps that he was holding up with one hand."

Mother and Father gave me their beauty, part silhouette, part shadow box. Part cleavage. Part Cheryl Crane. Part anger and remorse. Part failure. Part admiration of Diana Vreeland's will to redefine beauty. Part beaten-up Barbie doll. Part Al. Part sex, drugs, and Marilyn Monroe. I carry their beauty inside the very soul of my being. Dark, with shades of gray. Light, with storm clouds in the distance. Because of Dad and Mom, I'm not afraid to dream of dark victories and black beauty. I'm not afraid to be in love with the night.

ALL
MY THANKS TO
DASHING DAVID AND BEWITCHING BILL
VOLUPTUOUS KATHRYN, DIAPHANOUS CAROL, AND PATRICIAN SALLY
BREATHLESS JEAN
DOE-EYED DORRIE AND LONG-LEGGED ROBIN
AND CLASSIC KATE TOO
STUNNING BONNIE AND BODACIOUS BETH
RED-LIPPED
SANDRA AND WIDE-EYED JANICE
WINSOME EMILY, EBONY-EYED STEPHANIE, AND STATUESQUE LINDSAY
EACH MORE BEAUTIFUL THAN THE LAST

PERMISSION
ACKNOWLEDGMENTS

ABOUT THE AUTHOR

DIANE KEATON is the **New York Times** bestselling author of **Then Again,** which was named one of the ten best books of the year by Janet Maslin of **The New York Times, People,** and **Vogue**. She has starred in some of the most memorable movies of the past forty years, including the **Godfather** trilogy, **Annie Hall, Manhattan, Reds, Baby Boom, The First Wives Club,** and **Something's Gotta Give**. Her many awards include the Golden Globe and the Academy Award. Keaton lives with her daughter and son in Los Angeles.

www.dianekeaton.com
@diane_keaton
pinterest.com/keatondiane